WHOLESALING FOR QUICK CASH

WHOLESALING FOR QUICK CASH
A Real Life Guide to Flipping Homes

by Stephen Cook
www.lifeonaire.com

Legal Disclaimer

This publication is intended to provide accurate and authoritative information with regard to the subject matter covered. It is offered with the understanding that neither the publisher nor the author is engaged in rendering legal, tax or other professional services. If legal, tax or other expert assistance is required; the services of a competent professional should be sought (from a Declaration of Principles jointly adopted by a committee of the American Bar Association and a committee of the Publishers Association).

This book is intended for instructional purposes only. Every effort has been made to reflect the applicable laws as of the date of the publication of this book. However, this is a dynamic field of endeavor in which new laws are enacted, old laws revised and/or reinterpreted on a continuing basis and where statutes, rulings and precedential case law are constantly changing. Readers are advised to proceed with the techniques described herein with caution. Neither the author, printers, licensees nor distributors make any warranties, express or implied, about the merchantability or fitness for any particular use of this product.

ISBN: 978-0-9863228-6-0

Wholesaling for Quick Cash

A Real Life Guide to Flipping Homes

by
Stephen Cook

TABLE OF CONTENTS

Chapter 1: *Introduction* 7

Chapter 2: *Ethics and Morals* 15

Chapter 3: *Advantages and Disadvantages of Wholesaling* 23

Chapter 4: *How I Got Started* 27

Chapter 5: *Neighborhoods* 35

Chapter 6: *Building Your Team* 53

Chapter 7: *Real Estate Agents* 57

Chapter 8: *Private Lenders* 65

Chapter 9: *Settlement Attorney /Title Company* 77

Chapter 10: *Other Team Members* 81

Chapter 11: *Locating Opportunities* 95

Chapter 12: *Estimating Values* .103

Chapter 13: *Estimating Repairs* .109

Chapter 14: *Making Offers* 119

Chapter 15: *Offer Accepted, Now What?* 133

Chapter 16: *Marketing* 137

Chapter 17: *Buyers* 147

Chapter 18: *Closing the Deal* 155

Chapter 19: *Settlement Procedures* *163*

Chapter 20: *Controlling the Process* *173*

Chapter 21: *A Tale of Two Deals* *177*

Appendix A: *Glossary* *183*

Appendix B: *Forms*. *187*

Appendix C: *Credit Application* *199*

CHAPTER 1

INTRODUCTION

ABOUT THIS COURSE

Congratulations! You have separated yourself from the masses and taken your first step toward a more prosperous life by purchasing this course, which deals strictly with the topic of wholesaling (also known as flipping, assigning, buy low/sell low, etc.). I highly recommend this area of investing to anyone, particularly those investors at the beginning of their careers. It is one of the safest and quickest ways to start generating cash within a short period of time and requires almost no money. This course will provide you with all of the tools that you need to begin generating income quickly as a real estate investor.

My Background

My desire to invest in real estate had been burning for about 9 years. At the age of 19, I bought a copy of Robert Allen's Nothing Down as well as a number of other books on the subject. What particularly intrigued me was the idea of doing deals without any of my own money. Since I felt that I had given myself sufficient education to be able to complete a deal successfully, I began to look for opportunities. Subsequently, at the age of 21, I bought my first piece of real estate with no money down. But there was one problem. It was a restaurant, and along with the real estate I had bought a job. Of course, I didn't realize this at the time, and I felt proud of my accomplishment, happily going to work every single day. The happiness dissipated after about 6 months of working 80 to 90-hour weeks. Soon thereafter, I began to hate the place and was glad to sell out after another two months.

I must be hardheaded because I didn't learn my lesson. A few years later, I bought another piece of real estate with no money down at the age of 25. This time it was a $540,000 restaurant. Once again, I had purchased a job with my new investment, but this one was much better. I only needed to work 80 hours each week. How exciting. After almost two years I was tired of the whole mess and unloaded my restaurant to anyone who would buy it, taking a big loss. However, this time I realized that my "investments" weren't remotely close to investments. Both times, I had bought jobs that felt like prison. So, in the fall of 1997, I started over again. Having a steady paycheck and relieving myself of the day-to-day drudgery of running the restaurant was a very welcome alternative... or so I thought.

It didn't seem natural to me to have to show up for work, report to someone else and ask for my paycheck every week. The hours that I worked weren't much better than when I owned my restaurant, and the financial burden that was bestowed upon me from the short sale of my restaurant ate up every dime over and above what it took to pay my necessary bills. On top of everything else, my precarious financial situation continued to worsen as creditors from my restaurant began to track me down.

I felt a need to honor all of the obligations that I had personally guaranteed, so I worked out payment plans with all of my creditors. Though this provided some relief, by the time I came to terms with everyone, I didn't have enough left at the end of each month to make ends meet. My entire life was taking a turn for the worse, but I wasn't quite sure what to do. I knew only two things — I had to do something and I had always wanted to be a real estate investor.

Since the very first step to becoming or improving as a real estate investor is getting an education, I began seeking information. While it is true that I had a basic knowledge of no money down investing, there was a lot more to learn, including the mechanics of the various types of investing. However, one major obstacle stood in my way-1 had no money. Off to the Internet I went, searching for "real estate investing" and "no money down" and getting a bunch of responses. Within those responses, I discovered a robust real estate investing website. This site was nothing short of incredible. I was amazed by all of the information that was available to me, and even more astounded by the fact that it was all FREE. This was great because at the time, if they were charging anything for their information, I may not have been able to afford it, at least not immediately. I read everything on the site, and printed every single article and success story as well as countless posts from their news groups. For ease of review, I compiled all of this information into a binder and read it whenever I had free time. I studied that binder until I knew the techniques like the back of my hand. I participated on the news group day in and day out. I asked hundreds of questions. At some point, I was so well versed in the techniques that I could answer other people's questions. But there was still a problem...! had never done a deal.

It is sad, but there were many people in the same shoes as me. We all possessed enough knowledge to get started, but we also possessed fear. This fear was so overwhelming that it paralyzed us and prevented us from taking action. One day, a very personal experience lit a fire under me which was more important than my fear, and I went for broke. That fire, for which I will be forever thankful, changed my life for good.

After deciding to take the plunge, my fear was suppressed. I had no time to be afraid. Without another form of income, I had to succeed and therefore, however trite it may sound, failure was not an option. I believed deep in my heart that I was going to be successful, and I put myself on the same level as successful investors. The way I viewed it, if they could experience success in real estate, then so could I. They were human beings just like me — no better, no worse — and though I may have valued the knowledge they had gained, I didn't idolize them. I realized that they had just applied their knowledge and made something happen. Consequently, if I were to make something happen, then all I had to do was use what I had learned. This realization also laid bare the fact that if I didn't make it, the only person I would have to blame would be myself.

In my case, I jumped into the game as a full-time investor from the start, placing everything that I owned at risk come hell or high water. You can start part-time without taking such a risk, but your success will still hinge upon your efforts and yours alone. When all is said and done, you will have no one to blame for your failures but yourself.

Notice that I said before that my fear was suppressed, not gone entirely, and neither will yours magically disappear. However, you have to realize something. Any investor, new or seasoned, experiences fear, stress and anxiety whenever they push the limits of their knowledge and ability and venture into uncharted territory. These three forces are compounded whenever an investor pushes their financial envelope at the same time. However, no investor will ever achieve anything if they don't overcome their stress and anxiety and take action. Do they take action blindly? No. Neither did I and neither should you. First you need to educate yourself as I did in order to minimize any known risks. But, shortly after you've finished your education, you will need to step out of your comfort zone and chase your goal. Is success always guaranteed? Absolutely not. Is failure always guaranteed? Only if you don't take any action.

The process of learning to minimize risk through education and then taking action is the most important process you will ever undergo toward success as a real estate investor. It is one that you will repeat whenever you enter a new phase of your investing career, and put simply, there is no other path to success. While it is true that some people prefer to forego the education and jump in the water without looking for sharks, I am not one of them. Why waste precious resources fighting more sharks than is necessary? Will sharks appear after I'm in the water even if the coast is clear when I enter? Maybe. Maybe not. The key is to educate yourself and fight as few sharks as possible.

How much education is enough? That's a good question and one that only you can answer. It depends upon your prior experience as well as your financial cushion. With regard to experience, some people may possess most of the required knowledge already as a result of their background in their chosen profession. These people will require less education than someone starting from square one. With regard to finances, some people will be able to take more lumps than others. Those who are able to absorb more financial missteps can afford to be less cautious and maybe start without quite as much education than someone who is investing with money which they have struggled to save 6-12 months in order to begin their investing career. Regardless of personal financial situations, however, the one thing that everyone needs to realize is that most of your education will come from actually doing deals rather than from a book, course or seminar. Books, courses and seminars will teach you the basics with which you need to arm yourself before jumping into the marketplace. They will help you to avoid common mistakes that could be devastating to your investment career. They can also provide you with the knowledge that it took someone else years to acquire, thus cutting your learning curve drastically. However, after the education, whether you have $2,000 saved or $100,000 saved, you need to go out and make it happen.

Real estate investing has been great to me, and it can be great for you. It has changed my life and provided me with the freedom to live my life on my own terms according to my own values. Today, after investing for about two and a half years, I have been involved in the purchase and sale of approximately 550 houses. I started with absolutely no money and bad credit, but a burning desire to succeed. This desire eventually prompted me to take action and use what I had learned. None of the benefits that I have gained would have been possible without taking action.

MY QUALIFICATIONS

I have bought and sold about 550 houses in about 18 years. I have done everything from wholesaling, to retailing, to creating and selling paper, to being a landlord. I have made countless mistakes and I intend to show you how to avoid making the same ones. The experiences that I will be discussing in this course are real live experiences. I have personally tested or experienced everything that you will read or learn in this course, and I will provide you with as many details as I can recollect.

Over the years I have coached many of the nations top real estate investors and I continue to do so today. My primary focus today is teaching business owners how to build their businesses to experience an abundant life. I call it Lifeonaire. It's sort of like being a millionaire, but instead it is someone with an abundant life. My students are experiencing tremendous success and living incredible lives all at the same time. Come and check us out at *www.lifeonaire.com*.

ABOUT THIS COURSE

In this course I'm going to share my real life experiences with you. I don't give you hypothetical situations. There are many ways to invest, and there are many techniques for pulling off deals. The many ways to invest are certainly not limited to what I have experienced, but what I have done works. I can testify to it from my own personal experiences. So I encourage you to read it, learn from it, and apply it. You'll discover much more about investing as you experience the journey.

It should be noted that I wrote this course back in 2001 and while some of the information may seem dated, the concepts and principles are being used by the nations top real estate wholesalers, many of whom learned from this course. In the time of the internet, due diligence has changed, advertising has changed, but the overall concept of buying low and dealing with motivated sellers is exactly the same. Enjoy and prosper!

CHAPTER 2

ETHICS AND MORALS

Proverbs 10:9 - The man of integrity walks securely, but he who takes crooked paths will be found out.

IN THIS CHAPTER, I will discuss the importance of operating your business with integrity and professionalism, a point which I simply cannot stress enough. I refuse to advocate any investment practices that are unethical in any way, whether they are geared toward defrauding someone, taking advantage of uninformed people, or just plain deceitful. I wholeheartedly believe that you should be completely honest with all of the participants in your transactions, even if it means losing a deal. In the long run, your reputation as a person of integrity will allow you to participate in many more profitable situations than you will lose as a result of your dishonesty.

SIGN YOUR NAME WITH HONOR AND SETTLE EVERY SINGLE DEAL

Proverbs 22:1 - A good name is more desirable then great riches...

Toward this end, the first point that I would like to make is that as a professional investor, you should be honest with the seller about your position and sign your name with honor. Make every offer with the full intent of settling the deal. If you will not be able to settle on a property, do not present an offer at all. If certain circumstances need to fall into place before you can settle on a deal, present the offer, but disclose those circumstances upfront. Above all, be honest with the seller about your position. This policy has never caused me to lose a deal and even if it had, there have been plenty of other profitable opportunities for me as there will be for you. Sign your name to each and every contract with honor. Anybody can go make a bunch of offers, but your name is your name and it has value. If you sign contracts without producing, then in time your name will have little worth. People do not forget when someone backs out of a deal. Bad reputations catch up to investors, even in large cities. On the other hand, if you sign your name with honor, you will reap the benefits. As a result of honoring my contracts, I can offer less than other investors for a home in my area and have my offer accepted over other, higher offers because my name has worth. Sellers know that I will produce. Attaching this type of value to my name has not always been easy, but it has definitely been worthwhile.

My intentions when I first started investing were to wholesale properties exclusively. However, I have encountered several situations when I could not find a wholesale buyer and was forced to honor the contracts and settle on the homes myself. In fact, this is the only reason I ever started to rehab houses, and if you try to wholesale enough properties, there will come a time when you will be in the same position. When you come to that point, if you are signing your name with honor, you will find a way to settle on the property and rehab the house. If you absolutely want to avoid rehabbing and your intentions are to back out of a deal if you cannot wholesale it, I suggest that you put a clause in your contract which reflects this.

As I said before, it hasn't always been easy to settle on every deal. I have had a couple of occasions where settling on a deal seemed like it was going to blow up in my face. In both cases, I was able to put the deals together, even though they weren't great deals for me. I broke even on one, and made about $500 on the other. But the bottom line is that I settled them. I didn't wait for something to happen. I got out and hit the streets. I found buyers to step in my place. I didn't wait for the phone to ring, but rather I started looking for investors who were buying in the areas in which I had homes under contract and I started selling. In one case, I found a buyer the day before I was supposed to settle. Granted, we did file for a 4-day extension, but I marketed the home up until the last minute and found a buyer who settled in my place.

WEASEL CLAUSES - UNETHICAL AND UNNECESSARY

While we are on the subject of adding clauses to your contract, let me take this opportunity to discuss "weasel clauses." Such clauses say things like, "Contingent upon the inspection of my partner," when you don't have a partner or, "Contingent upon the inspection of my spouse," when your spouse has already seen the property. I completely disagree with the use of these types of clauses and believe them to be unethical, dishonest and totally unnecessary. Every single time you put your name on a contract to purchase a home, you should do so with the full intent of purchasing that home even if all else fails. Under no circumstances should you tie up someone else's property with the intent of walking away from the deal if you can't wholesale it to someone else, unless your contract contains a clause that clearly makes the seller aware of your intentions.

However, only those who are absolutely opposed to rehabbing a property should bother with such a "wholesale only" clause. For everyone else, why include a "weasel" clause at all? What protection are you seeking? Presuming that you've educated yourself to properly evaluate the "as-is" condition of a property, you don't need protection from anything else but the possibility that you might not be able to arrange financing. Such a situation may result from the condition, type or location of the property (if you've made your offer sight unseen) or from the fact that your purchase price is too high and you won't be able to borrow enough money to purchase and renovate the property. In either case, you can exercise your financing contingency, which is clearly disclosed upfront to the seller in your offer and, for the most part, the only contingency that you'll ever need.

I say "for the most part" because on occasion, there will be legitimate unknown factors which will require the insertion of a separate contingency because they can make or break a deal for you. For instance, suppose you are looking at a home that has a well as its water source. If the well is dry, you wouldn't be able to provide water for your new buyers and therefore you should include a contingency which gives you the opportunity to have a professional check out the well and releases you from the contract if it's dry. Similarly, you may be making an offer on a home specifically because it has extra land which you think you can subdivide. However, you need to check with your county to see if subdivision is possible. In instances such as these, you can clearly identify an unknown piece of information and need to insert a contingency giving yourself a chance to perform further due diligence before committing to purchase the property. Oftentimes, the seller will know or understand this.

Be careful not to confuse a legitimate contingency such as the ones used in these examples with a "weasel clause." The difference lies in the intent. The first intends to provide you with time to perform further due diligence, often on a particular aspect of a property, while the second serves only to buy yourself time to market the property and provide an exit if you can't wholesale it. Furthermore, even though a contingency such as "subject to inspection by my partner" can be genuine, once you learn how to inspect properties and estimate repairs, you won't need such clauses. In fact, as a wholesaler, you don't want to include them. In many cases, you will be buying most of your properties from banks and other institutions who reject offers with these types of clauses because they have been burned by them in the past. True, you may make some progress with private sellers (whether they are selling the property themselves or listing it through a Realtor), but even so, leave the weasel clauses out. If you've taken the time to educate yourself, they are unnecessary and your offers to these sellers will be stronger and have a better chance of being accepted without them.

In sum, my contract says Stephen Cook agrees to buy the property, and I make every effort to live up to my end of the agreement *every single time* whether I wholesale the property or not. So should you. If you can't flip a property to someone else, buy it. Don't run scared and back out. There are worse things in the world than fixing and retailing a house for a profit. Yes, I said profit. You've bought the property cheap, so you will make money, in spite of your mistakes, and add another skill to your tool chest to boot. Isn't this a wonderful business?

DON'T TAKE ADVANTAGE OF MOTIVATED SELLERS

Sellers can be motivated for a variety of reasons — medical expenses, a child's education, unpaid bills, unpaid taxes, divorce, pending bankruptcy, settlement of an estate, etc. — and the more imminent the reason, the more motivated the seller to get something done quickly. If you tell a motivated seller who must have $25,000 in two weeks that you will buy their home within two weeks, they feel an immediate relief. They start to make plans based upon that money. They make commitments that they expect to honor because they have placed their trust in you and feel that your word is good.

Now, what do you do in two weeks if you haven't been able to wholesale their home? Do you exercise your weasel clause, the one that says your partner, who is actually your dog, must approve of the purchase? What happens to the seller at this point? They can't live up to their obligations and commitments. Maybe they'll lose an opportunity. Perhaps their child won't receive a college education. Maybe they'll lose their home and get nothing. Maybe they will have to risk their life and delay a necessary medical procedure. Personally, I don't know how some people do it. I can't sleep at night signing a contract knowing that I'm going to stick the seller if I can't find someone else to buy the home. The moral of the story is not to take advantage of motivated sellers. It will come back to haunt you.

AVOID FRAUD

Real estate investing is a business that is becoming more well known for the fraud that takes place. The image of a real estate investor is slowly going from a glamorous title to that of a crook. It becomes very tempting at times to commit fraud to close a deal. Many times as a beginning investor you don't even realize that you are committing fraud. Someone else walks you right through the process. They have done it so often that they tell you, "Oh, this is OK, we do it all the time. Don't worry about a thing," and you just do it. Sometimes it doesn't even seem like a big deal, but it is. Telling a lender that you are buying a home for personal use as opposed to an investment so that you can get a lower interest rate or qualify for a higher loan to value is fraud. Giving a buyer a couple thousand dollars so that they have enough funds for a down payment, and not disclosing it to the lender is fraud. Marking up a purchase contract so the seller can give money back to you at settlement for repairs, and not disclosing it to the lender is fraud. These are scenarios that you will encounter regularly.

One time, I sat across the table from a loan officer who asked me to sign a gift letter for a buyer. I didn't give the buyer any funds to purchase, so I wasn't going to sign the letter. The loan officer's exact words to me were, "If you sign this letter, we'll settle next week and you'll walk away with $15,000. If you don't, this deal goes bust." I chose to let the deal go bust. If I can't do it the right way, I would rather not do it at all. Sometimes it's very hard to do the right thing, especially when no one is looking, but that's what having integrity and ethics is all about-doing the right thing even when no one is looking.

IS NO MONEY DOWN INVESTING ETHICAL?

Can you invest with no money down and keep your ethics intact? The answer to this question is a 100%, absolute, unequivocal "YES!" Many people find this difficult to believe because they feel that we are taking advantage of someone when we buy homes really cheap. In fact, I struggled with this issue myself when I first started, especially when it came to offering less than what a seller was asking. If they were asking $80,000, then offering $60,000 made me uneasy. But, after getting a few of these offers accepted, I realized that I wasn't the bad guy after all. Another example involves a woman who sold me two homes which had appraised for $100,000 (combined) for $29,000. She was crying when she sold them to me because she was so happy that I had taken them off of her hands. I realized then what a motivated seller was and that to them, I was truly providing a service. As a result of my experience, I have but one comment to make with regard to the sentiment that we are somehow stealing houses. **IF THE SELLER COULD GET MORE MONEY OR A BETTER DEAL FROM SOMEONE ELSE, THEN THEY WOULD TAKE IT!** Get over it! The reason the seller is willing to sell you their home really cheap is because no one else is willing to buy it or give them more for it.

Most of the properties that I buy really cheap are from banks or government agencies. Do you think they don't know what they're doing? Wouldn't they get more for their homes if they could? Would you feel bad if a bank sold you their home for 50% of FMV? If so, relax. It's all part of the business of finance and real estate. You are going to get paid for knowing how to buy and fix or buy and wholesale these fixer uppers. You will be helping not only the sellers by buying their homes which no one else wants, but you will help other investors by providing them with a profitable opportunity, the local community by doing something productive with an otherwise vacant home, and eventually a family by providing them with a nice place to live. All things considered, not only is no money down investing possible and ethical, but when properly practiced it provides the community at large with a number of benefits.

CHAPTER 3

ADVANTAGES AND DISADVANTAGES OF WHOLESALING

BEING A WHOLESALER IS not a job in which you have to report to someone else, however it is hard work. It is something that you will have to do regularly to make a living. It is more satisfying then a JOB? Sure, you are your own boss and you can make a good bit more money then with a JOB. Do you have to work 40 hours per week? No, but most likely you will. However, you will set your own schedule, perform the majority of work at home, and see your free time increase as you learn to integrate personal and work-related business. In short, you'll be working because you enjoy it.

One of the greatest things about wholesaling is that you don't need to bother with employees or any of the associated hassles, but you can make the income of someone with a thriving business. I've operated a number of businesses in which I had to manage employees, and I can assure you that not dealing with them is much easier.

Another advantage to wholesaling is that you have the opportunity to accumulate cash quickly. I have worked 10 minutes on a deal to make $1,000 and 15 hours on a deal to make $7,000. It used to take me 50 hours per week at a job for two and a half months, or about 500 hours, to make the same $7,000. My best wholesale deal to date took about 2 hours of my time and netted me $65,000.

Other advantages to wholesaling are as follows. You learn volumes about the business; you learn about opportunities in your local market; and you earn a very good income in the process. It can be used as your stepping stone to becoming a rehabber and, ultimately, to helping you put together a rental portfolio that will enable you to generate a lifetime of passive income. There is little to no risk involved as a wholesaler; you can start with no money; and you can do it on a part-time basis. You also control how much money you make per deal and the number of deals you do. If one a month makes you happy, then great, but if you want to do 10 or more per month, then you just have to increase your efforts. Another advantage is that unlike a real estate agent or an insurance agent, you don't need to be a fantastic salesperson to make good money — a good deal is a good deal. If your homes are priced right, then you can sell them to other investors whether or not you're a good salesperson. Of course, the better you become at selling and negotiating, the more money you'll be able to pull out of each deal, but this is true in any field.

As with anything, being a wholesaler does have its disadvantages. First, as a wholesaler, you have no passive income. You only get paid if you wholesale properties. If you want to take a vacation for a few months, you will not have any income for those few months. Second, you are not always able to wholesale a property and may end up rehabbing it to rent or resell. Third, the market is constantly changing, particularly in a hot area, and you need to keep abreast of those changes by tracking sales prices and talking to other investors. And finally, it takes some time to learn a sufficient portion of your market in order to support yourself as a full-time wholesaler. Don't expect to be able to go full-time overnight.

Now, I will admit that I started full-time overnight; however, I took the time to educate myself while I was still employed. Even so, by not finding another job, I placed an extraordinary amount of pressure on myself to perform. If I didn't succeed, I wouldn't have been able to eat or pay my mortgage, plain and simple. Worse yet, I would have had to go get another job to pay my bills and the thought of that disgusted me. To be honest, I think this drove me more than anything else. At any rate, I recommend that you do some serious soul-searching before going full-time overnight like I did. Only you can know when the time is right for you to make your move, bearing in mind that the "perfect" opportunity will probably never present itself and in fact, you may need to create it.

As you can see, the advantages to wholesaling outnumber the disadvantages by a fair margin and personally, I think wholesaling is the best way for someone to get their start in the business of real estate investing. In fact, it's how I got started.

EVOLUTION FROM WHOLESALER TO INVESTOR

I don't really consider a wholesaler to be a real estate investor in the true sense of the word. Webster's primary definition of an investor is "one who uses money, by purchase or expenditure, in opportunities with the potential for profit." This coincides with my personal opinion, that an investor is someone who creates, purchases or otherwise procures assets that generate a passive income. Since a wholesaler only earns an income if they work, in the strict sense of these definitions, a wholesaler is not an investor. Personally, I see myself as more of a real estate "dealer." After all, a car dealership does the same thing with cars as I do with real estate and yet they don't call themselves "car investors." On the other hand, some may say that a wholesaler is an investor since they invest their time into the business. In any case, the goal of a wholesaler should be to use the knowledge they acquire along with the healthy income they generate to become an investor who uses their assets to generate a passive income.

CHAPTER 4

HOW I GOT STARTED

Proverbs 14:23 – All hard work brings a profit, but mere talk leads only to poverty.

GETTING STARTED REQUIRES AN investment in yourself. No one, and I mean no one can just jump into the marketplace and start making money on a consistent basis by wholesaling properties without first gaining some knowledge. You need to develop knowledge about your neighborhoods, the investment climate, your local investors, the mechanics of a deal, etc. Educating yourself is the only way to gain this knowledge. You must spend time learning real estate terms, how to use forms, how to estimate repairs, how to construct offers, etc. Many people say that they don't have the time to learn. I can assure you that most investors, myself included, didn't have a lot of free time when they first started learning about real estate, but we all made the time to learn. My personal experience involved staying up late every night reading and listening to real estate tapes while I was driving, including tapes that I created by reading books out loud and recording myself. Every one of my "free" moments was spent studying real estate and investing. I say "free" because I made the time by sleeping less, forgetting about TV, and having lunch not alone but trading thoughts with other investors or maybe picking the brain of a Realtor. Oftentimes, I sacrificed my lunch hour altogether and met with attorneys, mortgage brokers, and other real estate professionals. Even now, I set aside time to learn about new techniques and grow in my knowledge of the subject. When all is said and done, the same rule applies to all of us, nothing works until we do.

Going full-time as a wholesaler is a major decision that someone has to make. While it is true that you can earn the same amount of money within two weeks that it takes months to make through your job, it may take you months to do your first deal, particularly if you are investing on a part-time basis. After your first deal, it may take you many more months to be able to wholesale properties on a consistent basis. The good news is that once you have the first deal behind you, they become much easier. The more deals you do, the bigger your buyers list will be, more neighborhoods you will know, the more private lenders you will encounter, and the better salesperson and negotiator you will become. In addition, you will get more offers accepted as your knowledge of your local market continues to grow. The reason for this is that as you become more familiar with local neighborhoods, you become more efficient at identifying deals. Soon you will recognize which ones are worth pursuing and which ones are not. In short, becoming a wholesaler is a learning process which depends upon the amount of time you dedicate to learning the business and the amount of relationships and credibility that you are able to establish with buyers, private lenders willing to finance your buyers and real estate agents who specialize in foreclosure properties.

Personally, I made the switch to a full-time wholesaler without ever having done a deal. This worked for me, but it was at times extremely stressful and challenging. I placed myself in a "do or die" situation and took my lumps. But I kept moving forward and never questioned my decision to leave my old job. In fact, I shut that door so tight that I had no choice but to move forward. I *had* to do deals just to survive. As I said, this worked for me. Your personal circumstances will dictate whether or not you are ready to go full-time. Overall, If you are working a job that is paying the bills and you are able to complete a deal each month, then most likely you will be able to double or triple your production if you become a full-time wholesaler. Whether or not you choose to fire your employer is up to you, keeping in mind, however, that if you don't perform, neither you nor your kids, if you have any, will eat.

BIRD DOGGING VS. WHOLESALING

Being a Bird Dog simply means that you work to find properties for an experienced investor. Find the property, line up the seller with the investor, and get paid if they do the deal. It just doesn't get much simpler than that. In fact, in many cases, you don't even have to negotiate the price with the seller.

The downside is that as a Bird Dog, you don't get paid as much as if you wholesaled the property yourself. For this reason, bird dogging gets a bad rap from many investors. However, I praise it. As a Bird Dog, you need absolutely no money or credit to get started in real estate, and you risk nothing. The only investment you make is that of your time, which is an investment that you'll need to make anyway as a beginning wholesaler in learning the same things that you'll learn as a Bird Dog.

Being a Bird Dog is how I got started. It is where I acquired the rest of the tools that I couldn't learn in a course or book. By being a Bird Dog, I had a risk-free opportunity to learn my market, how to determine good homes from bad homes, how much to pay for homes, how to estimate repairs, how to negotiate, what areas to buy in, what attorneys to use, where to get the money, etc... Much of the education that you will receive as a Bird Dog will be tailored to the specific area where you invest. This is one of the main advantages of bird dogging, as no book or course can cover the ins and outs of every neighborhood across the country. What I do in Baltimore, MD will be different then what is done in Macon, GA, or Columbus, OH or Seattle, WA. You can't use my title company in Texas. My hard money lenders won't lend in Delaware or any other state outside of Maryland. Repairs in Baltimore tend to cost more than in other parts of the country. Home values can vary greatly by neighborhood so formulas for determining what to pay for a home can change even within your own investing area. Granted, these are all things that you will learn as you begin investing yourself, but wouldn't it be nice to learn from someone already doing it in your area, someone who can save you time by teaching it to you so that you don't have to learn the hard way?

As a Bird Dog, I made $1,000.00 per deal. I did seven of these deals in two months. The money was OK, certainly enough to make a living, but the education was tremendous. During those two months, I acquired a little bit of money and a lot of knowledge, enough to become a Wholesaler.

Being a Wholesaler may or may not require some risk on your part. This is determined by where you are acquiring properties (we will discuss this later in the course). The primary advantage to being a Wholesaler over a Bird Dog is that you have an opportunity to make much more money per deal. My profits as a Wholesaler have ranged from $0 to $65,000 per deal. The longer I do this, the higher my average profit per deal climbs. Currently, I average about $10,000 or more profit per deal.

You may find out that being a Wholesaler is not the place to start simply because there can be some risk and some money required on your part. However, being a Bird Dog for a while will help you to overcome these obstacles. The good news is that it can be done. I know... I did it.

FINDING THE RIGHT INVESTOR FOR WHOM YOU SHOULD BIRDDOG

When seeking someone for whom you want to act as a Bird Dog, you should find a seasoned investor who does volume. If you deal with a rehabber who only does one or two rehabs per year, then you won't get much exposure to the market. In my area alone, there are probably 100 investors who do 20 or more deals per year. These are the types of people from whom you want to learn. They buy 2 deals per month on average, and if they had someone such as yourself finding them good deals, they might be able to do a third or fourth deal a month.

In addition to looking for an investor who does a lot of rehabbing, if you are going to learn something you want to make sure that your prospective mentor has some experience and a track record. You don't want to spend your time with someone who has a goal of 2 houses a month but is struggling to do one every 2 or 3 months. The reason I warn you about this is that some investors tend to exaggerate when discussing their activities. After speaking with them for a while, you'll find that their numbers are inflated and that they've done two rehabs, not three, and made $10,000, not $30,000.

TO INC. OR NOT TO INC.

Many beginners get all wrapped up in determining whether or not wholesaling (or flipping, assigning, etc.) is legal. Well, it is legal-in all fifty states, as a matter of fact.

The next decision is whether or not to incorporate. The answer is that at some point, you probably should. This is a business, after all, and in addition to shielding yourself and your family from personal liability, you'll want to take advantage of the tax benefits of owning your own corporation. Whether or not forming a business and incorporating is costly process in your state, I would suggest that your first action should be to locate deals. Once you have established that you can locate deals and make money as a wholesaler, then you can go through the time and expense of starting a company.

Since we all have different circumstances and plans for the future, everyone will have different needs and concerns. Therefore, before forming a company, you should express your needs and concerns to a competent attorney and accountant, preferably those who are used by other successful investors and ideally those who also invest in real estate for their own account. However, even the best accountants and attorneys hold different opinions on the same issues and you will also notice that the more people who you go to, the more widespread their opinions will be. It can be very confusing, but remember your goal is not to find the perfect tax strategy. As time passes, the accounting rules, tax laws, and your financial strategy will all change. Rather, the key is to find a competent attorney and a competent accountant with whom you feel comfortable, be sure they have good references and a track record of success and then place your trust in them. Do not be intimidated by this process, it is really rather easy. Millions of others have done it, so can you.

In addition to providing legal tax avoidance and protection from personal liability, establishing a company will give you credibility in time, provided that you follow through on all of your commitments. People will recognize your name and feel more comfortable dealing with you than with someone who is obviously just starting out.

I will not give any legal advice in this course, though I will tell you that 1 have chosen to operate my business as an LLC and an S-corp.. This structure allows me to make the most of tax savings while providing me with protection from personal liability.

REAL LIFE EXPERIENCE

As I mentioned before, I started out as a Bird Dog. My first few deals were deals that I found specifically for one investor. My agreement with him was that he would pay me $1,000 for each home I found that he bought. I would go out and look at dozens of homes per day. I stayed on top of the market and whenever I found a home that I could buy cheaply, I took it to this investor. In most cases, he made an offer and signed the contract. He cut me a check as soon as the offer was accepted. We did 7 of these deals in two months. Over the course of the two months, I put a little money in the bank, found a hard money lender, and became comfortable in submitting my own offers. The first deal that I wholesaled on my own the following month netted me $7,000. All told, within 8 weeks I had made $14,000. Within my first 3 months, I had made $23,000. Not too bad for a beginner. What I did, though, wasn't the result of some special talent or gift. With some time and effort, you can do it too.

Just a quick note on bird dogging. I highly suggest that every beginner start out as a Bird Dog. It isn't always possible to find someone to work for, but if you can, don't ever worry about how much the investor is making off of the deals that you bring to them. You will not be able to put a dollar value on the education that you can receive as a Bird Dog. In fact you will learn and still make money as you learn. How many places have you heard of that pay you to go to school? Working as a Bird Dog for a seasoned investor can cut years out of your learning curve. If you were thrown into the market with no knowledge, no contacts, no money, and no experience, it would take you years to learn what you can learn from a seasoned investor if you are observant.

CHAPTER 5

NEIGHBORHOODS

DECIDING WHERE TO INVEST is something that you will have to spend some time researching, especially if you are not already very familiar with your market. You will discover neighborhoods that you never knew existed. When I first started out I wanted to be the investor with the nicest properties in the nicest areas. } searched high and low for properties in my immediate surroundings and other neighborhoods near me. Hundreds of homes later, I had no luck finding anything and ft became pretty discouraging. I did come across homes in $140,000 neighborhoods that could be bought for about $120,000, and I thought they were great deals. Today, I wouldn't even consider them as something worth investigating.

In an attempt to help you determine those areas near your home in which you should be buying, I have come up with a Neighborhood Scale, presented on page *44*. This scale is a pictorial which ranks the different neighborhoods in the Baltimore area from the war zones (1) to the mega rich communities (8). There are opportunities everywhere on the scale, though I will say that it is more difficult to make money at the ends of the spectrum. Therefore, you will want to concentrate your efforts somewhere in the middle. It is up to you to find these areas in your community, educate yourself about them and determine how you are going to make money in them. They will provide you with your greatest success.

When referring to the Neighborhood Scale, keep in mind that many different styles of homes can be found within a particular ranking. The pictures that are displayed are only meant as a guide.

SAFETY WHEN INSPECTING HOMES AND NEIGHBORHOODS

One other thing that I'd like to stress is that you should always keep safety in mind when looking at homes. If you are going into an unfamiliar neighborhood for the first time, you may feel more comfortable taking a partner. At times, with or without a partner, you may be overcome with fear. If you ever catch yourself in a neighborhood that scares you, keep your car moving, get out of the area, and make a mental note not to look at homes in that neighborhood again.

You should also remain alert when investigating vacant homes. When entering the home, be sure to take a flashlight and a cell phone and watch your step. I've inspected some run down, dilapidated properties where I gingerly walked through, keeping an eye on the stability of the flooring, the stairways, etc. You should also be aware that, particularly in urban properties where the front and back doors aren't boarded, locked or nailed shut and/or the first floor windows are open, homeless people and stray animals may be calling the place their home. If you see that a property is not secure, you might not even want to enter. Just assume that the property needs everything and move on. Additional safety measures include mace or pepper spray in case you run into a stray animal, or leaving a list of the homes that you are going to visit that day with someone you know.

Keep in mind that none of this is meant to scare you. I've been in many, many homes and never had any trouble, but I did want to make you aware of what could happen. Just use common sense, be careful, and remember that if you ever feel uncomfortable, exit the home or the area as soon as possible. Your well being is much more important than any profits you may be passing up.

NEIGHBORHOOD SCALE - MEGA WEALTHY

Homes are usually very much In demand In the wealthy to mega wealthy neighborhoods. Typically, they are maintained very well and as a result, finding a distress sale is tough but not impossible. I once found a home in one of Baltimore's most desirable neighborhoods. It was a total wreck, but surrounded by homes that retailed for $500,000 on up. This home was listed at $125k and I pursued it, offering $75k. I figured that the property needed $250-300k worth of work to be in the same league as the others around it. Unfortunately, it was sold to another buyer for $100k.

NEIGHBORHOOD SCALE - WAR ZONES

On the lower end of the spectrum in the war zones, it is very easy to find homes really cheap. In fact, you can get people to give you homes in the war zones and in some cases, sellers are desperate enough to pay you to take the properties off their hands. Needless to say, these properties are not worth pursuing. Even if someone gives you a property, you have to pay taxes on it and you are responsible for upkeep, safety issues, etc... It is very difficult to unload a property in these types of areas. Unless you have a number of buyers who don't mind dealing in the war zones, then I would recommend that you stay out of them. It is much easier to wholesale a home in a good neighborhood then it is to give away a home for nothing in a war zone.

NEIGHBORHOOD SCALE - TARGET AREAS

These are the neighborhoods where you should concentrate your efforts. Typically, they fall between 3 and 6 on the scale and exhibit the following characteristics: 1) blue collar, working class demographics, 2) older (30+ years), having been around long enough to have properties with deferred maintenance, 3) property values in the bread and butter price range for your town or city, a range which is usually slightly below the average selling price of homes in your area. By way of example, here In Baltimore, where the average price of homes in the area is approximately $300,000,1 like to target homes that have retail values in the $150,000-$350,000 price range, and 4) established property values. You will find that investors will pay more for a home that has several valid comparable sates within a three-block radius than they will for a home that has only one rather suspicious comparable sale within a three-block radius. Generally, I look for comparable sales which involve one homeowner selling to another Investors tend to push the high-end of values when selling, and foreclosure sales transferring a property from a homeowner to a bank are useless. Similarly, I disregard sales transferring a foreclosure to a homeowner since they often reflect some sort of discount.

IT'S A WAR ZONE... OR IS IT?

It is important that you study the neighborhood scale and relate it to your local area. Some of us may consider neighborhoods that only rank as a 3 or 4 on the scale as a war zone, but truthfully, these are not war zones. They are areas which many investors-rehabbers and landlords prefer, and they fall within your bread and butter range for wholesale deals. As an investor, you can choose to disregard the 3 and 4 areas and work only in the better neighborhoods, but you will be leaving a great number of deals behind you.

There are even deals to be found in the neighborhoods which rank as a 2 on the scale. Typically, these are primarily rental areas on the fringe of the war zone. You should probably treat these neighborhoods as a secondary source of deals until you have more experience, and if you do decide to look for properties here, keep in mind that most landlords prefer cosmetic repairs to the pain and suffering of a total rehab. They want to start receiving cash flow as soon as possible with as little money out of their own pocket as possible. Since these are primarily rental areas, if you can't wholesale a property, your worst case tends to be fixing a property and putting a tenant into it yourself. If this is the case, you might still sell the property to a landlord after it is repaired. Many people would like to own rental property but don't want to go through the trouble of repairing one.

As with anything, the key to success in any of these neighborhoods is education. Talk to other investors and landlords in your locality and get to know which areas they like and which they don't Then use this information to buy homes. And don't worry if you haven't memorized your entire city. I discover new neighborhoods all the time, and so will you. Just start with one section of your city, learn it very well, and go from there.

As an exercise, it is a good idea for everyone to identify neighborhoods in your local area that fit into all the different categories on the scale. Once you think you've identified a neighborhood that fits into each category, go into the war zone number 1 and get out quickly, but drive directly to the number 2 neighborhood. Take note, how bad does the number 2 neighborhood look compared to what you just left? Then travel *to* the number 3 neighborhood. At this point, you may feel that you are in a pretty good area. The purpose the exercise is this — the quality of the neighborhood is a matter of perspective. People who live in the war zone think that neighborhood 2 is a really good area, neighborhood 3 is an excellent neighborhood, and neighborhood 4 is an upscale place (to live. As I said before, most of your deals are going to be done in areas 3-6.

Choosing a Target Area

In choosing a target area, there are a number of factors to consider. First, your target area should have neighborhoods in the middle of the scale, ranking anywhere from a 3 to a 6. It doesn't have to contain each of these types of neighborhoods, but it should contain one or more of them. Second, I strongly recommend that you choose a target area as near as possible to your home. If not, you will quickly find that working chosen area is very difficult as a result of the driving time required to get there. Third, you should limit the size of your target area. Find a few good neighborhoods on which to concentrate your efforts rather than spreading yourself too thin. The smaller the geographic area of your hunting grounds, the less time you will spend in your car and the more efficient you will become at identifying opportunities and locating resources. You will get to know the area better, and people (other investors, title attorneys, contractors, insurance agents, mortgage brokers, other team members, and the public at large) will get to know you. Before long, you will be made aware of deals before anyone else ever knows of them, simply because you are a presence within the area. You will not be able to establish this presence if you are spread too thin.

More advantages of choosing a smaller target area include the ability to develop a greater understanding of market values, so much so that you will be familiar with how the values of homes change from Mock to Mock, especially in more urban areas, you will know how well homes are selling in the area, and also the types of people looking to buy homes in the area. You will become familiar with market rents, and you will become aware of typical problems with homes in an area such as sewer line blockages or termites.

Once you know your target area backwards and forwards, you might want to consider expanding your area. Until then, be careful not to take on too much too soon. Ideally, you should be able to get to your target area within 30 minutes and refrain from targeting areas that are more than an hour away.

WILL THIS WORK WHERE I LIVE?

Many people question whether or not (hey will be able to wholesale real estate in their town or city. The answer is that it is possible to wholesale property anywhere. That is not to say, however, that I would be able to wholesale as many properties per year in Clarksville, VA (pop. 1500) as I do in Baltimore, MD. Therefore, the question becomes, "How many deals or how much volume can I do in an area within a given period of time/ and the answer to this question will vary with your individual circumstances. However, even if you did live in small town like Clarksville, you can still succeed in wholesaling. You just might need to: 1) dig deeper to find your sellers and obtain much more intimate knowledge about your sellers than I need to obtain in Baltimore, where I can scan the MLS for my deals and/or 2) consider wholesaling other types of real estate in addition to single family homes — commercial, multi-unit residential, mobile homes, raw land, or even small businesses, for example.

The concept of tying up property and collecting a profit for finding a buyer is the same regardless of the area in which ft is practiced or the type of real estate that is transferred. What you make of this idea, with or without the help of this course, is up to you.

TYPES OF HOMES YOU SHOULD BE SEEKING

Homes come in all different shapes, sizes, colors, and styles. Therefore, it is important to determine what types of homes are attractive to your wholesale buyers, whether they are rehabbers or landlords. Many beginners don't understand what a "real fixer upper" is. All to often this is one of the biggest hurdles for a beginner to overcome. The homes that I look at and think are in good shape are homes that some beginners feel are beyond repair, ready for the bulldozer Homes that stink and need the carpets cleaned and wails repainted are in super condition and usually not a prospect for the homes that I'm able to buy. I look for homes with holes in the roof that let the sun and rain into the home freely, floors that are warped caved in ceiling, 2 feet of water in the basement, stink that will knock you over from 20 feet away, broken windows, trashed kitchens, holes in the walls, graffiti everywhere, commodes that are stopped up and overflowing. This is what you should be looking at if you are looking for motivated sellers. I can assure you that the owners of these homes don't want them.

PROPERTY REQUIREMENTS OF A REHABBER

Every so often, I have run into fixer uppers that \ could buy really, really cheap in areas where homes were selling for good money. Upon further investigation, I discovered that the only reason I could buy the home so cheap is that no rehabber wanted it. Even after it was fixed up, the style of the home, the layout of the floor plan, or some other quirky thing was going to keep retail buyers away. As a wholesaler, you need to be conscious of the fact that rehabbers need to find homes that they can sell, the types of homes their buyers are seeking. They won't purchase homes that don't fit this profile, and neither should you.

There will be lots of minor advantages and disadvantages to the homes that you will find. Keeping in mind that even the least attractive homes can be a good deal at the right price, the purpose of this paragraph Is to point out those qualities that make a home more attractive to a retail buyer and thus to a rehabber. First and foremost is that a home should be in a safe neighborhood. You will have a hard time selling a home to a rehabber if there are other boarded up homes on the same block. Second, the property values in the neighborhood should be established, it is possible to sell homes in less stable, homeowner neighborhoods, but your rehabbers will be more conservative when estimating the after repaired value of the house and therefore your selling price as a wholesaler will be less than it would otherwise be. Third, a home should have at least three bedrooms. This is not to say that retail buyers don't buy two bedroom houses. In fact, in two of the higher dollar areas near the Inner Harbor in Baltimore, a 2BR home is very desirable and very easy to wholesale. Rather, my point is that in most cases, you will have a much easier time wholesaling a three or four bedroom house than a two bedroom house. Fourth, the layout of the home should provide for enough space so that the homeowner can use everything comfortably. If not, your rehabber is going to have a hard time selling the house. Finally, the last thing to consider is parking, People want to have a place to park their car when they get home from work, something which can be difficult on a narrow side street or busy main street.

Just like there are qualities that a home must have in order for it to be attractive to a rehabber, there are qualities that will make a rehabber avoid a house altogether. These are: screwy floor plan (walk-through bedrooms offering no privacy (unless they can be made private), bathrooms off of kitchens, bedrooms directly off of living rooms).

Neighborhood Scale			
Zone 1		Zone 5	
War zones, Many board ups. Trash. No pride of ownership. People will give you homes in these areas.		You begin to see much pride. There are few renters but they also take care of the homes and the yards. Good rehab area.	
Zone 2		Zone 6	
Fringe of the war zones. Many homes available in these areas. Usually too close to the war zone to attract homeowners. Mostly rentals.		Hard to come by renters in these areas. Rentals usually command top dollar. Tough to find fixer uppers but worth it when you can.	
Zone 3		Zone 7	
Mix of renters and owners. You begin to see pride. Lower income home buyers will buy here. Most of your rehab and resell opportunities will be here.		Very hard to flnd fixer uppers. The residents here can usually afford to take care of their homes. Retail buyers will pay top $ for fixer uppers.	
Zone 4		Zone 8	
Mostly home-owners but some rentals. Good first time buyer neighbor-hoods. Pride is evident. Greet rehab potential.		Deals are almost impossible to find. Most never will find one.	
The gray zones are HOT zones. This is where you should search for opportunities.			

Kitchens in the basement that can't be easily relocated to the first floor, extremely narrow bathrooms that can't be enlarged or rearranged, one or more low quality, amateur additions, low ceilings that can't be raised, sloping ceilings that make half of a room unusable, houses that are located on an alley, houses that are located among commercial buildings, or huge houses that need a ton of work, unless they are in an area where the values justify the effort. There are areas in Baltimore where the renovation cost of some homes exceeds their after repaired value.

You should also be careful with homes that are different from everything else in the neighborhood. I frequently find homes in the middle of a decent subdivision that are small, obsolete-looking shacks. How the home ever got there in the first pi ace is a mystery to me and probably everyone else living there. The rest of the homes in the neighborhood may be worth $200k or so, but such eyesores might not get $100k on their best day. When you encounter these types of quirky houses, be very conservative when estimating their value and be very particular about the types of properties that you use for comps.

Finally, one other thing of which you should be aware is that rehabbers tend to stay away from the totally dilapidated houses. Although they fix homes for a living, they prefer to deal with cosmetic rehabs as opposed to the "Money Pit."

PROPERTY REQUIREMENTS OF A LANDLORD

Landlords tend to be a little less picky than rehabbers when it comes to buying property, especially if they are focused on holding the property for the long-term. They might not mind a few board-ups on the block (as long as they aren't next to the property they are buying) and they might not mind a quirky feature such as a walk-through bedroom. As a landlord, they are mainly looking for properties that don't require a whole lot of work to put them in rentable condition which will allow them to start generating cash flow as soon as possible in a neighborhood where people want to live (in other words, maybe a 3 or 4 on the Neighborhood Scale but not a total war zone). And of course, the bigger the positive cash flow, the better.

The best way to determine the types *of* properties and areas that landlords prefer is to talk to the landlords and other investors in your town or city. Just ask them what areas and property characteristics that they avoid or seek and then avoid or seek the same things yourself.

MY REQUIREMENTS AS A REHABBER

I prefer to deal with smaller homes built after the 1950's with at least 3 bedrooms. To date, my experience with older homes has been that they cost me a lot more to renovate. The standards of construction were not as good before the 1950 s and older homes usually have more problems, especially the kind that you can't see. As a result, the cost of renovating them seems to be astronomical. I have taken a beating on two homes that I renovated which were 90+ years old. They both had a lot of unexpected damage, particularly structural, and 1 watched my expected profits of $20,000 per home plummet to about $5,000 with much of it eaten up in holding costs because the homes took so long to renovate. Experienced investors know that older homes pose more problems and will tend to stay away unless they are getting the homes so cheap they can't lose.

So whether you're looking to wholesale or retail a house, be careful not to buy an undesirable property. An example of this would be a home with a lot of additions. I have bought a couple of homes where the original owner had added many additions. I call these amateur additions. The job was obviously done by the homeowner themselves, since the work showed no professionalism at all. I figured what the heck. The home is cheap, so we can fix it. Well, all of the additions also created a lack of flow to the floor plan. Bedrooms were attached to the living room, and a bathroom was attached to the kitchen. I've had homes with a sun room with a ceiling that sloped from 6 feet to 5 feet in height making half the space unusable. I will no longer buy such houses unless I am getting them so cheap I could tear the whole home down and rebuild.

KNOWING THE END USERS FOR A PROPERTY

As you evaluate neighborhoods, you should be able to stand in front of the homes and visualize who the end user will be. If you are standing in front of properties that are going to be low income rentals in your mind, you may want to find a different neighborhood. On the other hand, if the property is in a homeowner neighborhood and the end user will be a family with children, then you are in the ideal neighborhood.

REAL LIFE EXPERIENCE ADVANTAGES OF A SMALLER TARGET AREA

Focusing on particular neighborhoods has allowed me to really learn the ins and outs of these areas. For example, I once purchased a home for which I had to replace the sewer line 2 weeks after tenant moved in. Shortly afterwards, I purchased another home on the same street and had to replace the sewer line there as well. My contractor determined that the original builder had used a very cheap product for their sewer lines and that most of the ones on the street are collapsing.

Now, 1 automatically include a new sewer line when I'm deciding what to offer on other homes in this neighborhood.

Another example of knowing a neighborhood involves a situation where I purchased *a* home without a basement. Including this house, I had purchased six homes in the same neighborhood. Four had basements, but two did not. Both of the homes without basements were infested with termites and I had to do major rebuilding to the foundations. The area was very close to water, and the ground was always damp. Without anything between the floor joists and the ground, they were very susceptible to those little wood-eating creatures. Now I know to stay away from homes without basements in this particular neighborhood.

REAL LIFE EXPERIENCE — FINDING MY FIRST DEAL

When I first started looking for investment properties, I lived in a county northwest of Baltimore City. The county in which I lived was fairly affluent and I had trouble locating deals, so I started traveling further to find properties to buy. My travels eventually brought me to Baltimore City and its surrounding neighborhoods. At times, I was traveling as much as an hour and a half each way to view a property. This traveling was not something that I necessarily enjoyed, but in the beginning I felt that it was necessary. Finally, after looking at hundreds of properties, I went out to look at a FSBO (For Sale By Owner).

The property was In a decent neighborhood. The complex in which it was located would have fallen at about 4 on the neighborhood scale, but the complex was surrounded by a neighborhood that would have been a 6. 1 wasn't sure what the home was worth and at the time, my method of determining value was to call other people who had homes for sale in the area (this is a no-no. t explain how to determine value properly in *Chapter 12: Estimating Values).* The seller of my subject property (the FSBO) was asking $70,000, which seemed like a fair price since I didn't know the value of other homes in the area. So

I began to construct an offer, using my cell phone to call the numbers on other "For Sale[1]* signs in the neighborhood.

On my first call, I got a Realtor by the name of Rob on the phone and asked the selling price of the property at 4 Chardon Court. He told me that the house was listed at $64,900, but that it was just reduced to $45,000. I thought. "WHOA! This is a hot deal."

"When can I see it?" I asked.

"Do you have the time this afternoon?" said Rob.

"I sure do."

• How about 3:00PM?"

I'll see you then," I said enthusiastically.

It was only 12:00PM at the time, so I ran to McDonalds to pick up some lunch and came right back to the home. I sat in front of it for 3 hours waiting for Rob to show up.) rehearsed over and over what I was going to say to Rob. I wanted to come across as an experienced investor. I didn't want anyone else getting the house before me. I really don't know what 1 would have done if someone else had come to see it while I was waiting, but the thought of telling them that I was buying the home and it was no longer available did cross my mind. No one else ever stopped to investigate and Rob arrived a few minutes after 3:00PM.

I was nervous *as I* got out of my car. "Hi, Rob?" is what I said as I reached out to shake his hand.

"Yes," replied Rob as he shook my hand and gave me his card with the other.

"Steve Cook" – said as I reached for his card.

Rob began telling me about the property as he tugged at the screen door. It was really stuck so he had to use both hands to pull it open. Then he retrieved the key for the front door from his pocket and opened it. "Whew!" was Rob's reaction as the door opened. I peered into the house and was shocked.

There was no carpeting on the floor, the walls were all different colors from pink to green to orange to yellow and blue. The house stunk to high heaven. Rob said, 'They (referring to the previous owners) had a lot of pets." I tried to lake everything in stride, but I was disgusted. I couldn't believe that I wasted so much time waiting to get into this dump. Though somewhat dismayed, I left open with Rob the possibility that I might still purchase the house.

The next morning, I had breakfast with a friend of mine who I had met at the local investment club meeting, I told him about the property and he told me to make an offer. My reaction was, "No way. The place is a dump," and went on to explain all of the work that was needed. He had a contracting background and said with confidence, "So it will take about $7,000 to fix it up. Make an offer."

I decided to take my friend's advice and make an offer figuring that there was no way they would accept. I offered $36,000 all cash with a $200 earnest money deposit and settlement in 90 days, writing it up using a contract I had bought from an office supply store. There was really no rhyme or reasoning to my offer of $36,000. I just seemed like a fair number based upon a drive-by appraisal of the property which Rob provided to me that estimated the value after repairs at $64,900. I wasn't sure what the comparable sales were, so I took this appraisal at face value and made an offer without using any sort of formula. Besides, I thought, they'll turn it down - which deep inside I really hoped is what they would do.

A couple of days later I received a call from Rob. He said, "The bank counter offered at $38,000." "Bank? What bank?", I thought. This was news to me. I had no idea that a bank owned the home.

I was actually relieved that they didn't accept my offer but counter offered instead. If they would have accepted, I would have been scared to death. Out of fear, I told Rob, I'll have to pass. I can't pay that much for the home." Rob sounded dejected, but it made me feel good to pass on a deal.

Later that week, I had breakfast with my friend the contractor again. I told him what took place He told me that I better go buy the home and that if I didn't, he would. 1 thought to myself that there was no way I was going to let this deal slip away. So I explained to him my fears, including the fact that I didn't have the money to close the deal. My friend told me that he would partner with me if I wanted to buy the house, so I agreed to do it.

Soon thereafter I called Rob back and said, "Rob, is the property at 4 Chardon Court still available?"

Rob replied, "Yes it is."

I boldly pronounced, "I've given it some thought and I think I'll take it.

"Great!", Rob said with a nervous enthusiasm, and we set up a time to wrap up all the paperwork.

When Rob and) got together 1 discovered that not only did the bank counteroffer on my price, but they also wanted me to take the property "as-is" without an inspection and settle in 30 days. Nor were they happy with the form of my contract and wanted more money for a deposit. Fear rushed over me again, I called my friend and he told me what to say.

I explained how our standard procedure was to have at least 60 days to dose, and that we never put more then $200 earnest money deposit down on a home. Rob called in another Realtor by the name of Jim, who ended up being the actual listing agent for the property. Rob was his assistant. Jim called up the bank and negotiated the terms right then and there. The bank accepted and I signed the contract.

My emotions were mixed. I was excited and scared, but I had a job to do. Eventually, though I had an opportunity to assign my contract for $2,000, my friend dissuaded me from making "only $2,000." As a result, I would end up rehabbing the home, living there for a year, and then selling it. Looking back, I should have taken the $2,000. Just as I say later in this course, until you have the financial capacity to take on a rehab, if you have the opportunity to wholesale a house, take the money and run.

REAL LIFE EXPERIENCE —WAR ZONES

One time, I decided to experiment on the fringe (a 2 on the Neighborhood Scale for my area) of the war zones. I bought a number of houses really cheap (i.e., less than $5,000) in areas which some would consider to be not the fringe of the war zone but the war zone itself. 1 did know that I wouldn't go into these areas at night, but I knew that there were investors who bought there so I figured, "What the heck. I'll give it a shot." Out of 10 homes that I bought for under $5000, I could only wholesale 5 of them.

Nobody was interested in buying the homes from me. I could wholesale homes that I buy for $50,000 and up much easier then I could the cheap ones, The moral of the story — stay away from the really bad areas.

CHAPTER 6

BUILDING YOUR TEAM

Proverbs 15:22 – Plans fail for lack of counsel,
but with many advisers they succeed.

ONE OF THE MOST crucial aspects of achieving and maintaining success as a real estate investor is assembling the right team. When it comes to investing, no man (or woman) is an island. It is absolutely necessary for you to work with others. I'm not suggesting partners, just business relationships with people who can help you as you help them.

You are the coach. As the coach, it is your job to put together a team of the best players available to you whose services you will require periodically. It will be important for you to develop a good working relationship with an attorney/title company, a Realtor, a mortgage broker, hard money lenders (a.k.a. private lenders), accountants, contractors, other investors, banks, advertisers, supply companies, etc. Chapters 7-10 of this course discuss the various professionals who you will want to have on your team. Section Two of this course, the Action Plan, will help you to assemble your team.

In assembling your team, you are going to have to meet a lot of people, ask a lot of questions, get a lot of referrals, and make choices. But beware. Do not assume that everyone who claims to know real estate will be able to help you. Not everyone will be well versed in what you want to accomplish. For instance, not every attorney who claims to be a real estate attorney can help you. The best way to find the best people for your team is to find out who other investors use. Do not be afraid to ask everyone you know that is already in the business. This is a very important step. As you meet other investors and their team members, simply ask them who they use for accounting, for appraisals, for plumbing etc... They may not always tell you, but if they do, it just saved you a whole lot of time. You will be surprised to find out how helpful most people will be (note: 1 did not say ALL people), and after a while, you will hear certain names over and over again. These are the people you want for your team.

Despite the foregoing, keep in mind that regardless of how careful you might be in selecting your team, you don't know everything, especially when you're starting out, and what sounds good when you interview a team member today may not sound good 6 months from now. As a result, you may have to change your team as time passes. Don't let this upset you. You probably won't be able to avoid it. Just consider it part of your learning process and move on.

RECRUIT LIKE-MINDED PEOPLE

When choosing your team, keep in mind that it is important that you work with like-minded people. You want the people on your team to have similar values and goals. Even though your team members may achieve their goals with different vehicles, everyone on the team should share common beliefs such as honesty, ethics, integrity, and a desire for win/win situations. I made a conscious decision to run my business with the highest level of morals and values and I expect everyone with whom I work to do the same. Keep in mind, though that try as you might you can't always decipher someone's values during your first visit with them, and consequently you may occasionally bring an undesirable member onto your team. But don't sweat it. You can always find someone new. After two and a half years I am still building my team, and it gets better every time I let someone go and make a new addition.

Proverbs 11:25 – A generous man will prosper; he who refreshes others will himself be refreshed.

It is common for many investors to expect Realtors, contractors, etc., to work for less money if they become regular customers. I do not advocate this. Your team will become the lifeblood of your business. Your relationships with your players will grow to a point where they can perform tasks without your interaction. Everyone should be compensated fairly for their services so that they will be happy to continue to work with you. For example, I do not recommend asking your Realtor to list your houses for less money or trying to beat your contractors out of a few hundred dollars. If they do a good job for you, let them get paid. If they get paid well by you, they will continue to want to work for you. If you start paying the members of your team less, they aren't going to want to work for you, and they will give their time to the clients who pay the most.

I see investors who use different contractors all the time, switch Realtors all the time, and hop from one attorney to another. All of this is time-consuming, unnecessary and very inefficient. With the right team in place, your business will run much more smoothly. The opportunity cost of finding and training new people is much greater than just paying a regular team member what they deserve for a job well done. In short, pay your team members what they're worth. The less you have to change that team, the better off you will be.

You should be fair to all of your team members in areas other than compensation as well. One of your main considerations should be that of team members' time. Don't expect them to do a whole lot for you without receiving anything in return, and don't expect them to work nights or weekends if you prefer to have those times off. It is OK to ask a favor here and there, but to keep someone on call all the time is a little much and you will be looking for replacements soon if this is the way you operate.

ALWAYS LOOK FOR NEW PLAYERS

Always be on the lookout for new and better players. You can never have enough people on your list of potential draftees. In time, others will be asking you for referrals and the more references you can provide, the more often they will come back to you.

REAL LIFE EXPERIENCE

When I find a good team member, I usually offer them incentives. I have been working with the same contractor since day one. We butt heads here and there, but overall he is a good guy and does a decent job. When I was first getting started and realized that my contractor just wasn't that bad I decided to do something that he wasn't used to hearing. He would always give me very low quotes to do work for me, and most of the time he came in below what I had budgeted. Well, he gave me a quote one time, and I asked him how long it would take for him to get the job done. I asked this because he never reached his deadlines. When he answered me, I told him that if he met his deadline, then I would pay him an extra $500 for the job. I showed up at the job the next day and there were 8 guys working on my house. I didn't know his crew was that big. He was used to having people tell him that they would penalize him if he didn't meet the deadline. I offered to give him a bonus — the exact opposite. This was a pleasant surprise for him and it created a loyalty that still exists today.

CHAPTER 7

REAL ESTATE AGENTS

IN MOST CASES, YOU will have to train a Realtor to work for you. Real estate agents are generally good at what they do, but most of them do not deal with investors and our methods are foreign to them. This does not make them bad people, nor does it make them stupid. Typically, an agent makes more money dealing with pretty houses and people with good credit, so this is the area where they become experts. If you can find an open-minded agent and teach them about what you do, then you can put together a mutually beneficial relationship. But first you have to respect the agent's perspective.

An agent gets their license and starts selling real estate to make a living. They aren't doing it for charity. They only get paid if someone buys a home and settles on it. A lot of work goes into a putting a deal together. Agents have been burned time and time again by investors who do not produce. Many so-called investors have real estate agents scour through listings, make appointments to see houses, show them around town, get them back into houses a second time, and never make an offer. Many investors who do make offers produce offers which are so ridiculous that if the agent knew this up front, then they probably would have never agreed to work with the investor. Then there are investors who get offers accepted but never settle on the deal. So the agent, who has about 30-40 hours worth of work into a transaction, will never get paid for their time. How many of you would want to go to work for a week and then not get paid?

WHAT TO EXPECT FROM YOUR AGENT

You need to recognize the fact that you are going to be looking at many houses and buying few. You don't need the agent to drive you all around town, pull up comps on every house you are going to see, or present offers on which you can't follow through. This is a waste of their time and yours. The only thing that I expect from my agents is to provide me with listings and submit my offers. Occasionally I will ask them to show me a home or pull comps for me if I can't find anything on my own. With few exceptions, you need nothing from your agent but for them to give you listings and submit your offers.

In terms of receiving listings, I expect to get updated listings at least weekly and sometimes daily, especially if I am in an active buying mode. I typically have them pull a list of fixer-uppers for me as well as a list of foreclosures. This list should include every single home that is available, not just the homes that the agent thinks are a good deal.

In terms of submitting offers, I go through every listing and in some cases look at every single home. Then I will make an offer on every single one of them regardless of the list price. I construct my offer based upon my formula and present it. It doesn't matter if they are asking $100,000 for a property and my formula tells me to offer $50,000. I offer $50,000 and the seller says yes or no. You need to make the agent understand that this is your strategy during your initial meeting as well as the fact that yes, sometimes a motivated seller will drastically reduce their price.

For example, I once purchased a home that was bank owned and needed a good bit of work. The bank was asking $93,500, but that was all the home was worth after it was fixed up. So I called the listing agent and told her that I wanted the home, but I felt the asking price was crazy. She agreed and told me that $93,500 was the price at which the bank told her to list it. Nevertheless, I told her to submit an offer on my behalf for $55,000. Lo and behold, the next day it was accepted. In fact, I was a little upset. They didn't even counter my offer, so I felt I could have offered less.

On another occasion, I offered $45k for a home and the seller (a bank) declined. A month later, I offered $40k for the home and the seller declined. A month later the seller reduced their price to $39,900, so I offered $34k and the seller declined. Two months later and four months after my initial offer, the seller reduced the price to $34,900 and I offered $29k. This time they accepted, taking $16k less than my original offer of $45k.

A third example involves a property that I bought for $1,000 which was listed at $35,000.

All of these were bank owned properties. It makes no sense to me why they do what they do, and I'm not going to try to figure it out. I'm just going to enjoy the good fortunes that come my way.

HOW TO FIND AN AGENT

When interviewing Realtors, you need to have a good idea of what you expect from them so that you can explain to them exactly what you need. They need to know exactly what their role is going to be if they are working for you. I simply tell new agents the following:

> *"I'm looking for a new real estate agent to help me, someone who can provide me with lists of fixer uppers and foreclosures on a daily basis. It won't be necessary for you to run me around town to see all of the houses. Occasionally, I may need to get inside of a home, but not very often. I may also need comps once in a while, but mostly I'll just expect you to submit my offers for which I will provide all of the terms up front. I will probably make about 20 offers. My offers will be low and most will be turned down, but I usually get one or two. Since you won't have to work to hard for these sales, would you be interested in working with me?"*

Most Realtors will say yes. The ones who usually decline are those who are mega producers and already busy enough.

It is not difficult to find a real estate agent, however it can be difficult to find one that you like who will also work with you. The first thing I suggest is for you to look for someone whose location is convenient for you. You will have to see them regularly and you don't want to be traveling out of your way all of the time.

GAINING ACCESS TO PROPERTIES

However commonplace it may be for investors to enter vacant homes, bear in mind that when you enter a property on your own without the permission of the seller (if it's a FSBO) or the accompaniment of a real estate agent (if it's a listed with a Realtor), you can be arrested for trespassing if the seller wanted to push the issue. Though it is possible that you will find an agent willing to give you the combinations to the lockboxes on vacant properties for the purpose of inspecting the property without their assistance, it is entirely within your discretion whether or not you choose to enter these properties on your own. I cannot recommend that you do so; however, I've never let this stop me.

When dealing with a new real estate agent, be sure to be totally honest with them. If you have never done a deal before, you shouldn't walk into their office and tell them that you are a successful investor who does 5-10 deals per month. First, this is lying, and second, your inexperience is bound to show through and you are sure to lose all credibility with the agent and anyone that they know. A real estate agent will be more inclined to work with you and be happy about it if they know everything about your situation up front. If you enlist their services through deception and they discover shortly thereafter that you have never done a deal, you will probably never hear from them again. Overall, real estate agents possess a good heart like anyone else, and they like to see people succeed. Moreover, they would like to be a part of your success story, so be honest with them and you will see how much further it will take you.

HOW TO WORK WELL WITH YOUR AGENT

The key to working well with an agent is for you to respect their time. Real estate agents are just like you and me. They do what they do to make money. Their time is money. If you have an agent run you all around town to look at houses, spend hours preparing contracts, hours on the phone with other agents, hours pulling comps (we will discuss comparable sales later in the course) and hours pulling listings but you don't buy a home, then the agent loses. They get nothing for all the time that they spent in good faith, hoping that you will buy a property. You need to be aware of this and respectful of it. Most investors who go to a real estate agent are beginners/wannabes. They never buy a home, yet the real estate agent invested a lot of time and effort into them. As a result, on the whole real estate agents have little success with investors and therefore tend to stay away from them. You have to be different. Be considerate of your agent's time and produce.

It is also important that you understand your role in relation to that of the real estate agent. All too often, investors expect real estate agents to do all of the work and to find them the good deals. If real estate agents knew how to find the good deals, they would buy them for themselves. It is your job to find the good deals. The only job of the real estate agent is to assist you by providing you with the information that you need to determine whether or not they are good deals.

DEALING WITH AGENTS IN GENERAL

There are a couple of strategies that you can pursue when dealing with agents. You can make your offers directly to the listing agent, or you can work with one agent who submits all of your offers on your behalf. The advantage to working with listing agents is that you may get them lobbying harder to get your offer accepted because they will get both sides of the commission. The disadvantage is that you will have to find out when these listings become available on your own. You should not have one agent provide you with listings and comps while using another agent to present your offers. This is unethical and will catch up with you in time.

I suggest looking for newer agents. Experienced agents tend to be set in their ways and unwilling to work with investors if they have not done so in the past. Most newer real estate agents do not make it through their first year as a result of lack of sales and, therefore, your business is always welcome. You can mold them to work well with you while at the same time providing them with the income they need to be successful and get over the hurdles of a beginning agent.

Some agents will ask you to sign a buyer's broker agreement, which essentially states that 1) if you buy a property listed on the MLS, it will be through them and 2) if you buy a listed property through someone else, they have the right to collect a commission from you. Whenever presented with this issue in the past, I always told the Realtor that I do not sign these agreements but rather will work with anyone who brings a deal to my attention. I go on to assure them that if they bring a deal to me, I will submit an offer on that property through them. However, if someone else brings a deal to my attention, then I will submit an offer through that agent. Furthermore, I state that I believe this is a fair policy and I will not compromise it. To date, no one has ever given me trouble after I explain my position. If they did, I suppose I'd find another agent. There are plenty of agents out there to help us in submitting offers. No sense in working with an uncooperative one.

CONCERNS OF A REAL ESTATE AGENT

Real estate agents need to make a living. They do not earn anything unless they sell homes. Whether they sell homes or not they have expenses that need to be covered and they can be rather costly. If a real estate agent is going to dedicate time to working extended hours with an investor, they are going to want to make sure that it is going to pay off. If you take up a lot of an agent's time but never buy a home, you can expect for the service from that agent to drop off significantly.

Real estate agents are people just like you and I. They became a real estate agent to make a living. Many become real estate agents in the hope of making a really good living. They are trained and taught to do their jobs well, however their training does not involve dealing with investors. Most agents are very good at taking buyers with good credit, and putting them into nice homes at top dollar. This is where they make the most money, and it is what they are taught how to do. When you approach a real estate agent you will most likely be asking them to do something that they have no experience with. Do not just assume that they will know what you are talking about. You need to be patient with them as they learn, and most likely they will need to be patient with you as you learn.

It is important that you have a good understanding of how everything is going to work out, and that you convey that to your agent. If you lay everything on the table up front then your agent will not be upset with you a week or two down the road because you were up front and honest with them.

REAL LIFE EXPERIENCE

I have never had a problem with finding real estate agents to work with. I can walk into any real estate agency, and find an agent to work with me. I sit down with the person on floor duty and ask them a couple of questions about their experience. I ask them if they are opposed to working with investors and I listen to their response. I then go into my pitch. I tell them that I am an investor and that I buy 3-5 houses per month. I ask if they would be interested in handling that for me. I always get a yes to that question. I then give them something else to get excited about. I tell them that I do not expect them to take me out to show me houses- their faces usually light up. Next I tell them what I do expect of them. I want listings on a regular basis and I want them to make all of my offers. I let them know that I will usually make about 30-50 offers per month in order to get 3-5 accepted. I ask them if that will be a problem. That usually is not something they like to hear, but they realize that they don't have to do anything else so they agree to it. I tell them that the reason I only get about 10% of my offers accepted is because I offer very low. I let them know that most will be turned down, but some will be accepted and those are the ones that we want. I also explain some of the things that I have learned when it comes to dealing with banks. Most banks pay real estate agents a minimum commission (as opposed to a percentage), so if you are making low offers your agent can still expect to make decent money. This is another plus, they like to hear that you want them to make money. Bring it up often- tell them that you value their time and you won't waste it. Be considerate and they will be loyal.

CHAPTER 8

PRIVATE LENDERS

DEFINITION

Private or "hard money"- lenders are private individuals with surplus money available for investment. Some have deep pockets while some have limited resources. Based upon their own personal criteria, they lend this surplus money, primarily on a short-term basis, to real estate investors who use it for a variety of profitable purposes including buying and repairing distressed properties.

TERMS

As you invest, you will discover that terms for private loans will vary from lender to lender and will depend upon the experience level of an investor as well as the length of an investor's relationship with a particular lender. Generally, a hard money lender will provide a loan for 50-75% of the after-repaired value of a home at an interest rate of 12- 18% for a period of six months to five years. They will also charge between 2 to 10 points as an upfront financing fee.

Other terms will also vary from lender to lender. Some will only charge interest, while some will amortize their loans. Some will lend repair money, others won't. Some will place the repair money in escrow to be drawn out as the work is completed; others will let you leave the settlement table with it. Some will lend closing costs, some won't. Some will even lend holding costs, though I have never personally met any lenders who do this. Ultimately, when finding hard money lenders, you will need to determine their terms and how they might fit into your plans as a wholesaler.

Like terms, lending criteria also vary from lender to lender. Each has their own preferences with regard to areas in which they will and will not lend and types of investors to whom they will and will not lend. Some will check your credit, some will not. Some will do their own appraisals, some will not. Some will charge for an appraisal, others won't. Some will charge an inspection fee for each draw from the repair escrow, others won't. Some will only lend in certain areas while others will lend everywhere. Some are more numbers-driven when it comes to decision-making while others go more on their feelings about you and/or the neighborhood.

ADVANTAGES TO THE WHOLESALER

As a wholesaler, you should strive to find as many private investors as possible. Hard money lenders are a great resource for all real estate investors (your buyers included), particularly beginners with limited cash and credit. Having several good hard money lenders in your pocket will help you to become more profitable. You will be able to act quickly and settle deals on time thereby enhancing your reputation in your marketplace. You will be able to obtain prequalification letters from your lenders, giving yourself more credibility when making offers. If you so choose, you will be able to take advantage of a rehab opportunity when it becomes available and obtain the funds necessary to do the repairs. You will be able to make offers with confidence. And finally, you will be able to act as the bank by connecting your wholesale buyers with your lenders so they can borrow money to buy prope. from you.

BECOME THE BANK AND MAKE MORE DEALS HAPPEN

There are two main reasons why you will need to find hard money lenders even if you aren't going to be buying any property. One is that you will inevitably find yourself with a property under contract that you can't wholesale, particularly as you are still learning the business. In this instance, since your intent as an ethical professional should be to settle every deal, it will be extremely helpful to have a stable of hard money lenders to call upon to finance the purchase and rehab of the property. However, even if you never have to settle on a property personally, the second and most important reason to develop contacts with as many hard money lenders as possible is that hard money lenders will be your best and most reliable resource in making sure that your deals are consummated.

Many prospective buyers for your wholesale properties are not all cash buyers, whether they claim to be or not. In reality, most cannot simply write a check from their bank account, but rather must borrow their money from other sources. Depending on their source of funds, this may or may not be OK.

If an investor doesn't have a legitimate source of funds, then it is your job to screen them a little further to determine if they qualify for you to take them to one of your hard money lenders. Many are capable of making mortgage payments and completing a rehab and would love to buy your properties if they could come up with the cash. In this case, it is your job to take control of the deal and lead them to the money. Become the bank as well as the provider of the property. But be careful. Maintain control of the transaction and use some discretion in deciding whom you take to your lenders. You don't want to burn bridges with your lenders by bringing them deadbeat buyers who default regularly. Your buyer's credit report should show an intent to repay all of their debts on time, and they should have some source of regular income which gives them the ability to make mortgage payments to your lender. For more information on qualifying buyers who call as a result of your marketing efforts, please refer to Chapter 16: Marketing. This contains a brief discussion of legitimate sources of funds as well as a questionnaire which allows you to quickly determine if a buyer has a legitimate source of funds and, if not, whether or not you will be able to take them to one of your hard money lenders.

Ultimately, you want to be able to take anyone who wants to buy a home from you (assuming they meet your minimum criteria) to one of your lenders. I have developed a regular following of investors who buy from me because not only do I find the properties but I also line up the financing, and you can too.

HOW TO LOCATE HARD MONEY LENDERS

Finding hard money lenders isn't really a mystery. At least it isn't a hard mystery to solve. You just need to get out there and take the right steps toward uncovering them. There are many different ways to locate hard money lenders, though when talking with other professionals, I tend to refer to my lenders as private lenders for the simple reason that everyone is not familiar with the term "hard money" lender.

I have found most of my lenders by asking for referrals from other investors, attorneys, accountants, insurance agents, etc., who are generally willing to help me because I do what I can to help them. Some of my favorite people to ask are settlement/closing attorneys. They usually prepare the loan documents for hard money lenders and most of them will be able to give you at least one name. In fact, on a number of occasions the attorney whom I asked was a hard money lender themselves.

ACCOUNTANTS

Accountants are a good source for hard money lenders for three reasons. First, many of them have clients who are sitting on a lot of cash and need to do something with it. Second, in some cases, they have clients who already hold paper. Such clients are great to approach about lending money since they already understand the business of lending. They have either taken back paper upon selling a property or they have lent their own funds to someone. Real estate paper is a very secure investment, and people who understand the business of lending don't mind doing real estate loans, especially when the LTV is low and the interest rate is high. Third, if someone trusts their accountant enough to let them handle their finances, then a referral from their accountant should carry a lot of clout.

HOME RENOVATIONS

Another method of finding hard money lenders is to write down the addresses of homes undergoing renovation. With few exceptions, if you go to the courthouse with ten addresses to uncover the lender involved in each of these renovation projects, you will find that a private lender is funding at least one of them. Contact the lenders that you discover and add them to your list, especially if they have already lent money on a home in an area where you want to invest.

INSURANCE AGENTS

Insurance agents who sell hazard insurance policies (particularly those agents who specialize in investment properties) must put a "loss payee" on all of the policies where a lender is involved. The lender is the loss payee, and of all the loss payees, the insurance agent can determine which are private lenders. An active agent could probably go through their records and come up with dozens of names of people who have lent money privately on property for which they have written policies.

MORTGAGE BROKERS

Mortgage brokers can also be a good source for locating hard money lenders, particularly those that work with investors on a routine basis.

Personally, I fell that any mortgage broker who deals with investors should have a hard money lender in their toolbox. If they don't, I wouldn't consider them to be a good mortgage broker. You may have to pay the mortgage broker a fee for the referral, but this is a small price to pay in return for getting a deal done.

LOOKING FOR LOOT IN ALL THE WRONG PLACES

Increasing your chances of finding a hard money lender has to do with the circles that you run in, the people you ask, and the number of people you ask. Chances are if you ask the cashier at your local Qwiki-Mart if they know of any hard money lenders, the answer you get is going to be, "Huh?" If you ask an attorney or title company who works with a number of investors in your area, it is much more likely that you will find someone who will be able to provide you with the names of several lenders. If you don't get anywhere the first time, don't stop asking people until you find one.

When seeking and communicating with hard money lenders, you must keep in mind that most are private individuals. They are not institutional investors who have a set standard of guidelines dictated by the Federal Reserve. As individuals, they are people just like you and I. They can be flexible or they can be tough. You can talk to them, befriend them, and laugh and joke with them. They can be your neighbor, your doctor, your attorney, or your bus driver. They usually don't advertise that they lend money, but instead are found through word of mouth.

QUESTIONS TO ASK HARD MONEY LENDERS

1) A blank questionnaire to follow when calling hard money lender can be found on the next page. Following are the questions on the questionnaire as well as the answers you can expect:
2) *What LTV do you lend up to?*
   Typically they will answer 50-75%. The more the better.
3) *Will you finance 100% of the purchase price?*
   Some will some won't, in many cases it depends upon the deal.
4) *Are there any areas that you won't lend in?*
   Some lenders do prefer certain areas.
5) *What are your terms?*
   Usually 12-18%, and 1-10 points
6) *Do you check credit?*
   Some do, some don't.
7) *Will you lend repair money?*
   Most of the lenders that I know will lend repair money.
8) *How much notice do you need to fund a deal?*
   Most can act quickly. I have received money from a Hard Money Lender in as little as 24 hours. In fact it was the first time that I ever borrowed money from a Hard Money Lender. I was supposed to settle on a home the next day when I finally got up the nerve to call the lender. I spoke to him for about 5 minutes when he agreed to lend me $41,000. It was enough to cover my purchase and closing costs. The lender personally dropped a check off with the title company the next morning.

9) *Will you lend money for closing costs?*
   Some will, some won't.

10) *Do you prefer to work with a certain attorney or title company?*
    Most lenders prefer to use one that they have used in the past.

11) *Is there an appraisal fee?*
    This is usually split down the middle. Some lenders charge appraisal/inspection fees, others don't. The bigger lenders usually see this as another profit center.

12) *Would you be willing to write me a prequalification letter that I can submit with my offers?*
    I have asked two lenders to do this for me and they were both happy to do it.

13) *If I locate the deals and bring my buyers to you, would you be interested in financing these buyers?*
    High volume lenders usually want all the business they can get. Lenders with limited resources tend to be more choosy with regard to whom they will lend money.

HARD MONEY LENDER QUESTIONNAIRE

Name: ____

Address: ______________________________________

____

Phone Number: __________________

Fax Number: ___________________

1) What LTV do you lend up to?
2) Will you finance 100% of the purchase price?
3) Are there any areas that you won't lend in?
4) What are your terms?
5) Do you check credit?
6) Will you lend repair money?
7) How much notice do you need to fund a deal?
8) Will you lend money for closing costs?
9) Do you prefer to work with a certain attorney or title company?
10) Is there an appraisal fee?
11) Would you be willing to write me a prequalification letter that I can submit with my offers?
12) If I locate the deals and bring buyers to you, would you be interested in financing these buyers?

PREQUALIFICATION LETTERS

As mentioned in Chapter 14: Making Offers, you will need a prequalification letter to submit along with your offers on many distressed properties, particularly those that are owned by institutions. You can obtain a prequalification letter from a hard money lender for this purpose, and in fact, your offers will carry more weight when submitted with a prequalification letter from a lender that is active in your area whom most real estate agents — particularly the ones that specialize in foreclosures - will recognize.

Be sure that you ask your lender for a "Prequalification Letter" and not a "Commitment Letter". A commitment basically locks them in, a prequalification letter gives them an out if they don't like the deal. Many newbies have contacted me about the difficulty they have had in obtaining a prequalification letter, and I based off of what they are telling me, I believe that they don't understand the difference.

Here is a sample of the text from one of my prequalification letters:

This is to confirm that you have been prequalified for financing for the purchase of single family residential home based on a 70% loan to value appraisal, but with no cash out. The prequalification is good for a period of 60 days from the above day and is renewable by mutual written consent.

As always, final loan commitment is subject to the appraised valuation by our appraiser.

Don't be confused by the term "hard money." It does not mean that this money is difficult to find or obtain. Quite the contrary, it is actually some of the easiest money to get. So why is it called "hard" money, you ask? Good question.

In the world of finance, money is either "hard" or "soft." Hard money has stricter terms and a clearly defined repayment schedule. Softer money has easier terms and a more flexible repayment schedule (e.g., debt service subject to available cash flow). In the case of private financing, the terms for hard money loans are exceptionally harsh with very low loan to values (LTV's), higher than market interest rates and a lot of upfront points. With terms so favorable to the lenders, most hard money providers are concerned primarily with the value of the property, placing less emphasis, if any, on the credit of the payer. They just want to know that if the payer defaults, then they will possess an asset from which they extract their original investment and possibly more. However, this is not to say that lenders desire to go through the hassle and expense of taking back and reselling a property but merely to point out that due to the terms of the loan, private lenders are secured, and feel secure, whether a borrower pays or not.

REAL LIFE EXPERIENCE

Currently, I have a list of about 25 private lenders who will lend money in my area. To date, I have only used 5 of them, using one of them for about 90% of the deals for which I or my buyers have needed financing. The reason I have chosen to use this one lender in particular is that he never runs out of money, he does every deal that I bring to him, and he is always strictly business. He is concerned about the home and nothing more — his rules stay the same. Many other lenders tend to be fickle, lending in some cases but not others, and this doesn't work well for me, especially when I'm doing a lot of volume. I need a lender who produces every single time.

CHAPTER 9

SETTLEMENT ATTORNEY / TITLE COMPANY

A COMPETENT REAL ESTATE ATTORNEY will be an important asset to your team. In addition to being able to provide you with referrals of realtors, lenders (private and conventional) and accountants, a settlement attorney can be very instrumental in creatively structuring a deal when the need arises. For this reason, you should choose your settlement attorney carefully. Remember that even though an attorney or title company may be accustomed to doing real estate settlements, this doesn't mean that they know how to bring a creative deal to fruition. Given time, many of them can figure it out, but you don't want to be their guinea pig. Find out which attorneys other investors in your area are using and check them out. You will discover that the more active the investor, the more credible their attorney.

NOT ALL ATTORNEYS ARE CREATED EQUAL

In selecting an attorney or title company, you will find that, like real estate agents, not all of them are created equal. Many people simply assume that a settlement attorney is just that, and therefore they are qualified to handle your deals. This just isn't true. Some are more qualified than others and some give much better service than others. In addition, not many settlement attorneys work with investors. As you meet other investors, you will notice that most of them use the same attorney or, if you come from a highly populated area, that you will be able to count all of the attorneys used by investors on one hand. There are several good reasons for this. One is that due to the creativity that some real estate transactions require, investors like to use an experienced attorney. No one wants to be a guinea pig, teaching an attorney how to do your business, unless it's absolutely necessary. Another reason is service. Some attorneys are downright lousy, even those with a lot of experience. Be sure to select an attorney who is going to pick up the phone when you call and return your messages in a timely manner.

The bottom line is don't reinvent the wheel. Talk to other investors and pick an experienced attorney with whom you feel comfortable who provides good service. Your investing experience will be much more pleasant.

EXPECT GOOD SERVICE

Just another word on service. Some attorneys are very disorganized — not a good thing in a paper intensive business. Some do things last minute, make mistakes frequently, or just seem overwhelmed. Some do not return phone calls, and some are just downright rude. If any of your prospective settlement attorneys show any of these characteristics, avoid them like the plague. Find someone who provides good service as well as quality work, and here's why.

In addition to making your normal settlements proceed as smoothly as possible, a good attorney will take your calls immediately if they are available and return messages promptly. You should also be able to rely on your attorney to move quickly or take an urgent call when necessary. Likewise, the possibility exists that you will find a deal which needs to be closed as soon as possible, and you should feel comfortable knowing that you have an attorney on your side who can, and will, make the necessary arrangements and close the deal in a matter of days if need be. Of course, you shouldn't make a habit of rushing your attorney to close deals (check with them to see how much time they would prefer and how fast they can move if necessary so that you know your limits when negotiating), but here and there it may be necessary to move really fast in order to take advantage of a good deal. Above all, remember that regardless of how much respect you may have for your attorney or their knowledge, you are still the client. Expect good service and if you don't get it, take your business elsewhere.

PRICING

Here's some good news. Irrespective of their level of experience, most title attorneys will price themselves within a couple hundred dollars of each other. For this reason, I don't worry much about their pricing as long as my deals are getting done without a lot of hassle, and neither should you. Most attorneys will charge about the same amount for a settlement with a difference of only $250 between the high and low pricing in my area. So don't get too hung up on the costs and place your emphasis on receiving good service.

SEEK EXPERIENCE

Experienced attorneys can save you from your inexperience. When I first started out as a wholesaler, I knew the basics. I didn't know every step involved in seeing a deal through, nor did I know all of the different methods of doing a deal. Luckily, I encountered a couple of very experienced attorneys who have been through just about every kind of deal that there is. They taught me a lot. Sometimes I would bring creative deals to them to settle. I thought I had done well in structuring the deals only to have them tell me a better way, a way that would make me more money. Sometimes I structured deals that couldn't be done and the attorney took the time to figure out a way to get it done. These are just a couple of reasons why you want to draw upon the experience of attorneys who have been around for a while.

CHAPTER 10

OTHER TEAM MEMBERS

FOLLOWING IS A DISCUSSION about all other the other team members who will help to make your investing career a successful one.

CONTRACTORS

A good contractor will do quality work and complete a job according to schedule at a reasonable price. They will show up on time and finish the job rather than leaving it ninety percent done. Keep in mind, however, that just because a contractor is good at one thing doesn't mean he is good at all things. In fact, be wary of those contractors who say they can "do it all." Some can, but many cannot. Some contractors prefer to do just one thing since that is what they do best. In any case, I highly recommend that you check referrals of contractors. You'll likely be sorry if you don't.

Even though you may be concentrating on wholesaling, building a list of reliable contractors is essential. In addition to performing work for you if necessary, they can help you determine your repair costs and be available for referral to your buyers who might not know where to go for a particular repair. As we will discuss in Chapter 17: Buyers, the more you can help your buyers, the more likely they are to come back to you. For instance, if you find someone who is installing carpet and padding for $8 per yard, you had better get their name and pass it along to all of your buyers. They will save a few hundred dollars on every investment property and thank you for it. Or say that you sell a home that needs a furnace to someone and they don't know who to call. You are providing them with more of a service by providing them with the name of a good heating contractor. Always be on the look out for quality, professional contractors. Chances are high that someone you know will be able to use them.

GENERAL

A general contractor is what many rehabbers prefer. Having one person to call for everything is much easier then trying to keep up with a bunch of different subcontractors. They usually cost more, but the time you save in having them monitor the whole job is well worth it. General contractors are also experienced in the areas that we are not. If a general contractor is paying a subcontractor to do some work, then typically, the general contractor will want to get their money's worth and will make sure that the job is done correctly. As real estate investors, we may not know if a job is being done right. Even if we do, our time is better spent chasing deals than babysitting subcontractors. Therefore, a general contractor is well worth the extra cash.

HEATING, VENTILATING AND AIR CONDITIONING (HVAC)

As a rehabber, I can safely say that the heating systems must be replaced in about half of the houses that I purchase. For this reason, it is very important for a rehabber to be able to call upon a good heating contractor. When you find one whose prices are low, be sure to get their name so you can pass it on to your buyers. About half of the homes that you wholesale will need new heating systems.

ESTIMATED REPAIR COSTS

Typically a HVAC company is going to charge anywhere from $35-70 per hour to come out and do repairs. If you ever need to have the unit for a heating system replaced, you can expect to spend approximately $1200-$3200. At the lower end of the range, I have replaced gas forced hot air furnaces for as little as $1200 while new gas steam boilers have cost me as much as $3200.

Pricing for Heating Systems Repair / Replacement:	
Forced air furnace (gas or oil)	$1,200-1,800
Hot water boiler (gas or oil)	$1,800-$2,500
Steam boiler (gas or oil)	$2,500-$3,200
Oil tank removal	$500
General repairs	$300-$1,000
Central air repairs	$300-$1,000
Central air replacement	$1,000-$2,000
Central air duct work	$1,500-$5,000

PLUMBERS

Many of my renovations need some type of plumbing work. In most cases it is very minor and a handyman can take care of the job. But some homes have old galvanized pipes which corrode and reduce water pressure and I need to tear out all of the lines and install new copper piping throughout. For a job of this magnitude, you will want a licensed plumber. More important than minor plumbing work or even replacing old lines is the one area which causes me the greatest problems in older homes — clogged drains and sewer lines. You should know who is the best drain opening company in town. Be careful because many of them will come out and immediately tell you that you have to replace your sewer line because they want the bigger job. In my experience, I've called two drain openers to come out every time I have a clogged line and every time, the same one tells me that I need a new line. The other one comes out and is able to clear the line for me in most cases.

Estimated Repair Costs:	
Hourly	$35-70
Entire re-plumbing of home	$1,500-$7,000
Replace sewer line	$1,500-$5,500
(Note: the deeper the line and the longer the run, the more this will cost)	
Sewer line cleanout	$150-$350
Hot water heater	$350-$750
Hot water heater (do it yourself)	$250
Well Pumps	$350-$700

WINDOWS

In many areas, there are companies that specialize in replacement windows. I replace windows in about 80% of the homes that I renovate. Yes, it is necessary, and no, they aren't cheap. I have new windows fully installed for $200 each, a number which may vary in other parts of the country. Find out the best supplier of replacement windows. Your rehabbers will appreciate it if you can save them $25 per window, especially when they have to put 20 new windows in a home.

Estimated Repair Costs:	
Replacement windows	$150-$300
Glass replacement	$30-$100

FLOORING

Carpeting isn't cheap, but you can get a wide range of pricing for the same product. Find out who works with investors in your town and determine if they have special pricing for investors. On average I can save about 25% over the lowest retail pricing in carpet stores by dealing with a company that specializes in corporate accounts.

Hardwood floors are beautiful and usually too costly to redo for low-end rehabs. On the other hand, in upper scale homes, hardwood floors add to the value of a home and therefore I will refinish hardwood floors, but only in my nicest homes.

I usually assume that I will be putting new vinyl flooring in my kitchens and baths. If the bathrooms have good ceramic tile on the floor, then I'll leave it alone. Otherwise, new vinyl goes down. Vinyl flooring is cheap and it adds tremendously to the appearance of the home.

Estimated Repair Costs:	
Carpet cleaning (minimum 5 rooms)	$30-$70 per room
Carpet with installation	$9-$15 per sq. yd.
Refinish hardwood floors	$1.50-$2.50 per sq. ft.
Vinyl floor replacement	$2-$4 per sq. ft.

ELECTRICIANS

Many older homes may need to have the electrical service updated. They may not have grounded outlets, and they may still have fuses instead of circuit breakers.

Rehabbers will want to make sure all of the homes have updated electrical systems in order to pass inspections and meet the electrical needs of the new buyers.

Estimated Repair Costs:	
Upgrade service (breakers and amperage)	$800-$1,700
Rewire entire house	$3,000-$6,000

KITCHENS AND BATHS

These are probably the two most important areas when dealing with renovations. Most of the homes that I have purchased have had outdated kitchens and bathrooms. What many people perceive to be expensive fixes are really relatively cheap. Money spent renovating kitchens and bathrooms is what gets a rehabber their best returns.

Estimated Repair Costs (Kitchen):	
Cabinet replacements	$700-$4,500
Countertops and installation	$150-700
New sink and fixtures	$200-400
Total Kitchen Renovation	**$1,500-$5,000**

Note: While you can spend more than $5,000 on a kitchen, you can have a basic kitchen installed for between $1,500 and $2,000.

Estimated Repair Costs (Bath):	
New vanity, sink and cabinet	$200-$500
New tub enclosure	$200-$500
New tub and surround	$300-$1,000
New toilet	$200
Total Bath Renovation	**$700-$3,000**

Note: While you can spend as much as $3,000 on a bath, you can have a basic bathroom redone for between $1,000 and $1,500.

PAINTERS

Painters are needed on every renovation. It helps to have a list of good painters that you can refer to your buyers. Painters usually charge by the square foot or by the room. The pricing from one contractor to another can be very wide.

By the square foot	$1-$4/ sq. ft.
By the room	**$100-$400/ room**

This is an area where the skills of painters can vary drastically from one crew to another. A good crew can do very detailed painting, and lot's of trim work. They typically cost MUCH more. We really don't need such skilled painters for the homes that we renovate.

Estimated Repair Costs:	
Paint interior	$150-$250 per room
Paint interior (do it yourself)	$30 per room
Paint exterior	$1,000-$5,000
Paint exterior (do it yourself)	$300-$1,000

Note: Cost of exterior painting will vary with size of home and condition of existing surface.

LANDSCAPERS

Landscapers can do a variety of tasks from cutting grass to hauling trash. Many of them can repair walkways, cut down trees, tear down old sheds, etc. Though landscaping is a cost that many people ignore, cleaning and hauling trash and cutting down trees can be a very costly expense. I have spent as much as $1800 to clean up a lot, cutting down all the overgrown bushes and trees and hauling everything away, and the lot was only 4/10 of an acre. In general, I budget about $400 for landscaping and trash removal.

ROOF / GUTTERS

The amount that you will spend on a roof will depend upon the type of roof (flat rubber, pitched shingle, pitched slate, etc.), the size of the roof, and the extent of the repairs required. In my area, it costs about $700 to lay a new flat roof on a small home and about $175-$200 per square (100SF) for a new layer of shingles on a larger home.

Gutters can be expensive or inexpensive to replace, depending upon the type that you use. They can be bought in pieces and assembled, but unless this is done carefully and the seams caulked properly, the finished product has a good chance of leaking. When replacing gutters, I prefer to install the seamless variety, which run me about $3 per foot.

SIDING

In my area, siding is an expensive proposition, particularly if there are no existing soffits. New siding can cost between $3,000 and $5,000 for a standard 1200SF home.

Therefore, many rehabbers prefer to paint the exterior of the home rather than install vinyl siding unless they are in a neighborhood where most of the homes have siding already.

SHEET ROCK

In my area, it costs about $25-$35 to install a 4' × 8' piece of sheet rock, depending on the amount you are having installed. Many times, gouges, holes and other marks on walls and ceilings can be repaired rather than replaced. Likewise, different textures can be sprayed onto ceilings and sometimes walls to cover imperfections. When estimating repairs, use your best judgment and when in doubt, assume replacement rather than repair.

BANKS

Like every other resource, you should stay abreast of the climate in the local banking community. Find out who is working with investors, what types of loans they are doing and what rates and terms. You should also know who is doing unseasoned refinances so your buyers can pull their cash out of a property and buy another one from you. These are the types of things that will keep your buyers in business and coming back for more. In addition, one day you will find this knowledge useful when you yourself want to use these banks.

ACCOUNTANTS

It is not necessary for you to have an accountant to get started, but you will need one when tax time comes. When you do look for one, it is extremely important that you find an accountant who understands real estate investing. I would suggest finding an accountant who invests in real estate themselves since many are weak when it comes to understanding real estate investors. I learned the hard way.

Newspapers / Advertisers

In addition to needing advertising salespeople for your own purposes, they are great to refer to your buyers. As I said before, many of the people to whom you eventually sell your properties will be novices and any type of assistance that you can provide them will be of benefit. Again, the quicker they get one deal done with you, the quicker they can buy another home.

MORTGAGE BROKERS

Be really careful when talking with mortgage brokers. They will all tell you that they can do everything, that they produce all the time, that they won't waste your time, that their processors are great, and that they have relationships with the underwriters and are able to get difficult deals done better than anyone. In reality, very few of the hundreds of brokers that I've met have really done a good job without wasting my time. I suspect the reason for this is that most mortgage brokers haven't been brokering loans very long. They were doing something else just a few years ago and, even without any experience, decided to become mortgage brokers. However, the industry boomed as a result of low interest rates and these people with no experience whatsoever were selling mortgages. In many instances, they learned at the expense of the consumer.

Even a good mortgage broker will have an extremely hard time arranging financing for your buyers through institutional financing. In fact, it's nearly impossible.

As a result of all of the controversy regarding "flipping" being talked about by the media, most institutional lenders have come up with new guidelines that prevent investors from quick turning their properties. The majority of institutional lenders will not provide funding to borrowers in cases where an assignment of contract or simultaneous close is involved. In fact, if you are selling your property within a year of purchasing it, lenders are backing away from the deal. If you ever hear anyone talk about "title seasoning," it is usually in reference to flipping a property in this manner. Unlike hard money lenders and most local banks which don't require any title seasoning before financing a new buyer, institutional lenders are requiring 6-12 months seasoning on the part of the seller before they will finance a new buyer.

So why bother to have a good mortgage broker on your team if they can't finance the people who buy your properties? Good question. Well, first of all, some mortgage brokers will be able to take you to private lenders or local banks who will finance or refinance your wholesale buyers. Second, even if a broker can't finance or refinance your buyers, it pays to have a competent mortgage broker in your bag for those wholesale investors of yours who may have a retail buyer for their homes but don't know where to get them financed.

Mortgage brokers are also very useful in helping you to stay on top of the activity in the mortgage markets, which is important. By keeping yourself informed, you will know the current trends and any obstacles that your investors might be facing. For example over the course of the last 2 years, more people have bought homes then ever in history; however, it is also probably the most volatile environment that investors have ever seen in the entire history of lending money, even going back to early biblical times.

It has not been uncommon to get a loan commitment for a buyer only to have it withdrawn because the program that existed yesterday no longer exists today. Neither has it been uncommon to get all the way to the settlement table with a deal only to see it fall apart at the table because the lender backed out.

The moral of the story is that there are a lot of mortgage brokers out there. Sift through the pretenders and find a good broker, an experienced professional who can give you plenty of references.

INSURANCE

Since many insurance agencies aren't willing to write policies on vacant investment properties, obtaining insurance on these properties is not always easy and it can be costly. Always make a note of the names of insurance brokers that you uncover who work with investors and investment properties. This can be a dealsaver when your buyer shows up at the settlement table without insurance because they weren't able to find an insurance carrier willing to write a policy on a vacant investment property for them. If your buyer is using his own cash to purchase the property, then this isn't necessarily a problem. However, if a lender is involved, private or institutional, they will want the property to be insured. In this case, you can call and ask one of the insurers on your list to write a binder and fax it to your settlement table. They can do this pretty quickly in an emergency, the problem is solved and you look like a hero.

OTHER INVESTORS

Maintaining working relationships with other investors is something that you should always work toward. I know of people who feel that every single person is their competitor. Consequently, they won't refer a single person to you nor will they work with you on deals. Their attitude is that this is a cutthroat business. In reality, there is more business out there than any one investor can handle, yet these foolish investors forsake all of the benefits they might gain by networking in a ridiculous endeavor to corner the market.

I help other investors all the time without ever expecting anything in return. Even those who are unwilling to help me or other investors receive my assistance because I believe that you should always offer help when asked — unconditionally and regardless of the actions of others. For instance, I have provided assistance to investors who will call or e-mail me for help, even though they won't give me the name of a mortgage broker or a contractor with whom they openly claim to have experienced success. However, I don't understand why they won't share this information. One way or another I'll find the resource that I'm seeking, so they aren't hurting me. Rather, they are hurting the mortgage broker, the contractor and themselves. The mortgage broker and contractor lose potential business and the investors lose profits from future deals or relationships from which they will be excluded as a result of their attitude.

Remember, though, to be sincere when helping people. Don't expect things in return. Otherwise, your help is insincere and your fake sincerity will be recognized as such, damaging the very relationship you are trying to build. Help other investors freely and sincerely and you will be pleasantly surprised to find that other investors will help you, sometimes when you least expect it. They can be some of the biggest players on your team in referring people to you, buying homes from you, lending money to you, bringing deals to you, bringing other buyers to you, partnering with you, etc. By burning your bridges with other investors, you lose all of this. So remember, friendly competition is a good thing. If you have no competition, chances are there isn't any opportunity.

I firmly believe in the saying, "What comes around, goes around." In my own life, I feel as though I have witnessed this dozens of times. Therefore, I believe that you should always do unto others as you would want them to do unto you. This philosophy may cause you to get burned here and there, but in the long run, you will come out way ahead. And even if you didn't, in my opinion, I would rather be broke and have lots of friends than make a lot of money and have everyone dislike me.

CHAPTER 11

LOCATING OPPORTUNITIES

YOUR PRIMARY GOAL AS a real estate investor is to locate money-making opportunities. As a wholesaler, these opportunities will arrive in the form of distressed properties, a type of investing which is very safe and can be very lucrative.

DISTRESSED PROPERTIES

Distressed properties are properties that someone owns but does not want for a variety of reasons. The property may need work, it may be a foreclosure that a bank does not want, it could be an estate sale with a half a dozen siblings who can't agree on anything, or it might be owned by a tired landlord or an out of state owner who can't manage their property. The bottom line is that the seller doesn't want the property, and you as a buyer are coming to their rescue. You will be looking for properties in these types of situations, particularly single family homes.

Personally, I have bought homes in move-in condition at wholesale prices and I have bought homes on the brink of being torn down at wholesale prices. In every instance, there was something that chased the retail buyer away. In some cases, it was a problem as small as dirty carpeting or old, peeling paint. In other cases, the home was clearly waiting for a wrecking ball and the owner knew why no one else wanted the home.

JUNKER HOMES

Most but not all of the distressed properties that you buy will be junker. These homes will look and smell bad. You will find homes that have burned down, homes with holes in the roof, homes that smell like cesspools, homes filled with trash, homes with rotted floors, homes with broken and/or boarded windows, homes infested with roaches or termites, homes with deteriorating walls, homes with crumbling foundations, etc. Do not be scared of these things. Later you will find out how cheap most of these repairs are to make.

The reason that most of your purchases will be junker homes is that these houses scare away retail buyers (i.e., owner occupant purchasers who pay top dollar for a home). Once a home does not appeal to the retail buyer, it automatically drops to the wholesale market. In the wholesale market, there are far fewer buyers than in the retail market. Therefore, you stand a much better chance than a retail buyer to get a property at your price, a price which leaves enough room for you to make a profit and for your buyer to make a profit when they retail the home.

VACANT HOMES

When looking for wholesale prospects, I'd like to stress that you should be looking for VACANT homes. Out of the 550 properties I have bought over my career, only a handful of those properties had someone living in them and most of them should have been vacant. If you find yourself constantly looking at homes that are occupied, chances are that you're looking at the wrong homes to pick up for a wholesale deal. In my experience, the most motivated sellers are those people who have vacant homes, mainly because vacant homes can only be trouble. Nothing good can come out of a home sitting doing nothing. They deteriorate, get vandalized, cost money in taxes, cost money every month in mortgage payments, etc. — a bad situation all around, and one for which you should be looking.

Distressed situations, junker homes, vacant homes — they all point to the type of person you are seeking, the motivated seller. Problems, whether related to the property or the owner (and possibly both), cause a seller to be motivated. Your opportunities arise out of these situations because you can provide a solution that benefits both you and the seller. This is why it is important to deal only with sellers who are motivated, and the bigger their problems, the more money you can make for there will be fewer people with the creativity and patience to find a solution. While it is true that some sellers will be more motivated than others, if a seller isn't motivated at all, they are a waste of your time. However, this is not to say you shouldn't keep in touch or at the very least leave them with a way to contact you. Time has a way of changing everything and sometimes a non motivated seller becomes a motivated seller almost overnight.

Motivated sellers are not hard to recognize once you know the type of person that you are seeking. Also referred to as "don't wanters," some examples of motivated sellers are banks, divorced couples, heirs to an estate, tired landlords, out of state owners, etc. The sellers with the highest degree of motivation are willing to do anything to sell you their property. With regard to wholesaling, most of the motivated sellers are banks who need to unload the properties that they own due to federal banking regulations. Oftentimes, their problems are compounded by the fact that the properties need more work than a retail buyer is willing to do, so the properties fall to the investor market.

Occasionally, you will run into FSBO properties that need a substantial amount of work and the owner is willing to take a big discount just to get rid of the property which has been nothing but a headache for them. Personally, I have bought about 90% of the properties that I have wholesaled through Realtors and the remainder from FSBO's.

HOW TO ATTRACT OR LOCATE MOTIVATED SELLERS

There are several areas in which I have had success in finding motivated sellers. Personally, my first and primary source of properties is through the MLS. Realtors have more properties available through the MLS than any other source and I have chosen to take the easiest route for the bulk of my properties. I usually have my Realtors print me a list of all foreclosures for the areas in which I am buying. Sometimes the list has hundreds of homes, other times it is down to a dozen or so. I also ask for lists of fixer uppers, and a list of updates, which contains all new homes that have been listed since a particular date. But setting aside my experience with the MLS for a moment, I have purchased properties by many other means, all of which are described below.

CLASSIFIEDS

I also scan the classifieds (online and in print) for opportunities. I have bought a number of properties by calling on an ad in the paper. It never hurts to call on an ad to see what someone else has. In fact, many times your conversations will become helpful learning experiences in which you and the advertiser can pick each other's brain, especially if the advertiser is another investor.

FARMING

This is a commonly used term for cultivating an area. When you farm a particular neighborhood, your goal is to turn up every opportunity.

You want every single person in the neighborhood to know that you are buying homes there. By placing signs throughout the neighborhood, sending postcards, dropping business cards, advertising in local papers, leaving door hangers, etc... you can pull more deals out of an area. In time, you will make yourself a household name within the community and anyone who has a home to sell will think of you. If a home becomes vacant, a neighbor may call you or someone will refer you to a friend who wants to sell their home, even before they place it on the market. Farming allows you to concentrate on a smaller area than you otherwise would, and the more adept you become at solving real estate related problems, the more deals you will be able to farm. Whether or not these deals will be wholesale candidates or other profit-making opportunities (commercial deals, "subject to" transactions, lease options, mobile home parks, rental property, raw land, etc.) depends upon your area, but what I can say is that there is more opportunity within 15 minutes of your own residence than you can imagine.

ADS

Running "I Buy Houses" ads is another effective way to find properties. However, don't be discouraged if you aren't buying homes right away. I purchase about 1 out of every 20 homes from people who call on my ads. As you grow as an investor and increase your ability to negotiate other types of deals (lease/options, "subject to" deals, deals involving owner financing, etc.) as well as improve your knowledge of local property values, your ratios will improve. Soon you may find yourself buying one property for every ten calls your ad generates. The ad that I run reads as follows:

Quick Cash for homes*Any area*Any cond*(xxx)xxx-xxxx

Classified ads tend to be unpredictable. One week you can get 10 calls on your ad, the next week you may not get any. Then the next week you can get 30. The key to running a successful ad campaign is to have your ad running continuously in your local papers. I have found that I get better results when I run my ad every Sunday without lapse. Don't expect to run one ad and have more properties then you can handle. In advertising, repetition is the key.

In terms of where to run your ad, most people recommend that you advertise in the major metropolitan papers. I have found that I generate more calls from the smaller publications. Obviously, I'm not getting to the population at large, but I am getting more bang for my buck. Web advertising that directs people to your website is an extremely effective method as more and more people are using the internet over print advertising.

As a wholesaler, you will be doing a lot of advertising, some for buying property and some for selling property. You should be running ads regularly if not every day stating that you buy houses. You should advertise in as many places as your budget allows since the number of phone calls that you receive will be directly related to the number of spots where your ad appears. Consider shirts, hats, pins, signs, and any other medium you can imagine. Be proud of what you do and let the whole world know that you buy houses.

REALTORS

Realtors are a fantastic source for properties. They have more properties available to them then anyone else. At any given time there can be tens of thousands of properties listed on the Multiple Listing Service (MLS) in your area. Depending on your area of the country, you may use realtors for 95% or more of the properties you buy. Even if this isn't the case, you will be able to find some deals among the thousands on the MLS. As you continue to make offers, you will begin to discover which properties to target and how to play the system in your area. After dealing with the same Realtors for a while, you start to get a feel for whom they represent and whether or not you are wasting your time with a low offer. However, the good news for beginners is that for the most part, there still isn't really any rhyme or reason as to what sellers will do. Therefore, even a beginner can play the numbers game to their benefit, get some offers accepted, and make money.

You will also find that the biggest banks in the country (the ones with the most real estate owned, or REO's) list all of their homes with real estate agents. Because of the sensitive nature of the banking industry, it is written in the corporate charters of most banks that all REO's are to be listed with a realtor. This is done to make sure that the properties are offered in a competitive environment, generating the highest sales price for the bank. In other words, the bank does not want their REO manager discounting houses to friends and family when a higher offer may have come in from someone else. So if REO's are what you want to target, you will have to establish a good relationship with a real estate agent.

SHOULD I BECOME A REALTOR?

Being licensed has its advantages and its disadvantages. The two biggest advantages for us as investors are direct access to property listings and direct access to comparable sales information. Furthermore, you can submit your own offers and collect a commission check for every house that you buy and sell. If you are doing rehabs, you can list all of them on the MLS yourself and save on commissions. Finally, you might be able to earn a commission check by helping buyers that you encounter with a home even if they don't want to buy one that you own.

Two of the main disadvantages to obtaining your license are the time required for classes and continuing education and the expense involved in terms of dues, fees, and insurance. If you aren't doing many deals or making much money, then I think being licensed will work against you. However, if you are doing a fair amount of wholesale deals a year, then having your license may begin to pay off. The bottom line is that whether you have your license or not, you will be able to succeed as an investor. You will need to weigh the pros and cons and make your own decision.

CARDS, FLYERS AND SIGNS

Passing out "I Buy Houses" business cards has also been an effective form of advertising for me. People usually hold onto these cards for a long time and pass them along when they know of someone in need. For this reason, I hand out cards everywhere, and I always make sure to give them to those who have bought a home from me. They know that I perform and become very good testimonials.

You should leave your business cards everywhere you go, too. So many investors tend to hold onto their business cards, reasoning that they shouldn't waste them. Well, having them sit in the box in which they were purchased is a big waste of money, mostly because they aren't making you money as they should.

Business cards, flyers, and signs are all cheap and effective ways of generating leads to purchase homes. Leaving cards or flyers on the doors of vacant houses has worked for me. I haven't done it much, but I've received calls from the owners of the properties when I have done it. This is a strategy that could probably generate many more leads for me; however, I've gotten lazy and don't like to stop my car to get out to leave a card.

CHAPTER 12

ESTIMATING VALUES

ESTIMATING THE VALUE OF a home after repairs are completed is a simple yet important step in calculating the price you want to pay for a property. All that you need to do to arrive at a value is to investigate the sales prices of similar homes or "comps"- in the same neighborhood. This isn't hard, just time consuming, particularly if you are working in an area where all of the homes are built differently.

WHAT EXACTLY IS A "COMP"?

"Comp" is short for comparable sales. When determining the value of a home, an appraiser uses recent sales of comparable homes to come up with a realistic value for a subject property. Typically, a good comp is a similar home that has sold within the last 6 months. By "similar" I mean homes that are close in proximity, have sold recently, and are similar in size, style and construction. You don't want to compare a two-year- old, four bedroom, two bath brick home with all the amenities to a three bedroom, one bath frame home built in 1930 that needs updating. Although both of these homes might be in the same neighborhood, they are not comparable. At a minimum, the homes you are comparing should have the same number of bedrooms and approximately the same square footage, give or take 100SF or so. While it is true that appraisers can make adjustments for square footage on an appraisal, this isn't an exact science. Therefore, if you want to be confident in your own estimate of the value of a particular property, you should stick to comparable sales involving properties that are roughly the same size. If you can't find homes that are very similar to your subject property, you will need to make adjustments to your values. We will go over this when we discuss appraisals.

When I pull comps, I usually go back 4-5 years so that I can also see trends in the values of homes in neighborhoods. And believe me, although we have been in this housing boom, there are areas that have been dropping in value. I know. I own a couple of homes in those types of areas.

You must become efficient in determining the value of homes, and therefore comps are very important to your success. The smaller the area in which you decide to work, the faster you will learn the property values and the easier it will be for you to stay on top of the market. For the area in which you specialize, in time you will only be checking comps to get an update on which way values are heading in a particular neighborhood.

SOURCES FOR COMPARABLE SALES INFORMATION

There are many different ways to obtain comps. My local newspaper posts recent sales in every Sunday paper. My state's tax records, which include the most recent sales price of every piece of property in the state, are available on the Internet. My real estate agent (and yours) has access to the Multiple Listing Service which can generate comparable sales from all the listed homes which have already sold and are similar to your subject property. Should you choose to get, or if you already have, your real estate license, you will be able to access this data directly. Websites all over the Internet provide you with sales data by street, neighborhood, zip code, etc. Certain information services provide comparable sales data to their users for a fee, sending updates at regular intervals (usually quarterly or even monthly). Whichever way you choose, you will need to have a consistent, reliable source for obtaining recent sales information so you can determine the after-repaired or "subject to" value of a property before you are able to construct an offer. This source of recent sales information will be particularly useful and necessary when you are learning a new area.

BLOCK TO BLOCK

If you are working in a major city, it is extremely important that you become very knowledgeable with the home values. Home values where I invest in Baltimore can go from $50k to $150k for the same home only two blocks away. It is very important that you determine values for homes in such areas with comparable sales as close as you can get them. Two or more blocks in some cases can cost you a lot of money.

APPRAISALS AND THE APPRAISAL PROCESS

An appraiser accesses different databases such as tax records and the Multiple Listing Service to find comparable sales for a subject property. Typically they look for properties which are the most comparable in size, style and age to the subject property. They will also want these properties to have sold within the last 6 months and be in close proximity to the subject property. Then an appraiser does a comparison of each home to the subject property noting items for each comp such as condition, size, number of bedrooms and bathrooms, additions such as garages, decks, amenities such as thermal windows or central air conditioning, updates, size of lot, etc. Taking all of the advantages and disadvantages for each comp into consideration, the appraiser looks at all of the comps at once and assigns values to them based upon how they stack up against one another. Eventually, the appraiser will choose the three properties which are most comparable to the subject property and will usually take an average of the three to arrive at a value for the subject property. Finally, the appraiser will incorporate all of his findings into a written report, one of which is included at the end of this chapter for your review.

You should know that appraisals are not an exact science. You can order 5 different appraisals for the same home and get 5 different values which vary greatly. The reason for this is that an appraisal is based upon the opinions of an appraiser, and each appraiser is going to have different opinions. Specifically, each appraiser will use different comparable sales, and each appraiser will have their own ideas about the condition of the property. On top of this, appraisers can also be swayed by the sales price of a property, particularly if the property is under contract for a specific price and the lender and/or mortgage broker are ready to proceed with the loan.

Other factors that are considered are days on market, condition of home, noise levels, amount of traffic on the street (residential properties on main streets are worth less than those in quiet neighborhoods), type of heating, proximity to schools, energy efficient items such as thermal windows, updating, additions, parking areas, garages etc...

ALWAYS CHECK THE VALUES YOURSELF — DON'T TAKE ANYONE'S WORD

It is very important that you position yourself to check home values on your own. You will spend a lot of time when you first start getting to know the true value of homes in a neighborhood. However, once you know the values, you won't have to spend the time learning them again. Never, I repeat, NEVER take anyone else's word for the value of a home. I took other people at their word in estimating the values of homes in an area and I got burned both times.

REAL LIFE EXAMPLE

One example is when I found a Cape Cod in a really nice neighborhood. The home needed a little work and all the homes on this block were the same, but none had sold in years. There were Cape Cods ail over this neighborhood but none were the same style, size or construction. I couldn't determine the value quickly so I asked my Realtor. She asked another person in her office who blurted out that he knew the neighborhood really well. He said the homes were worth about $120k. I felt that was a little high — my personal estimate was about $100k-but when he said $120k, I thought my estimate was conservative.

I went forward and paid $48k for this home which needed quite a bit of work. Estimates for repairs were about $20k. When I tried to wholesale the property, I quickly found out that the homes were only worth about $80k and that I had paid way too much. The home didn't have a basement, and it wasn't made of brick like the other homes in the neighborhood. Homes in the neighborhood had a reputation of shoddy construction, and were considered very small.

I was terribly upset with myself. I didn't have an out with this one because I made a cash offer with no contingencies, and I had to figure out a way to get it done. Ultimately, I sold the home with owner financing and no money down to a couple with really bad credit, and then I sold the note to a private investor. I didn't make any money on this deal. In fact, in addition to all my wasted time and effort, I lost about $1000. That hurt. It was my first big mistake, and I want you to learn from it. **DON'T EVER TAKE SOMEONE ELSE'S WORD FOR THE VALUE OF A HOME. ALWAYS DO YOUR OWN DUE DILIGENCE!!!**

CHAPTER 13

ESTIMATING REPAIRS

ESTIMATING REPAIRS IS NOTHING more than inspecting a house, taking down some general information and then adding up some numbers. It isn't any more complicated than that. This chapter will provide you with everything you need to get started.

YOU CAN'T GET INTO A HOUSE

If you can't get into a house, don't worry, no one else can either. Just assume that everything needs to be replaced and move on to your next offer. After inspecting enough homes, you will become proficient in estimating repairs to within a few thousand dollars without even getting inside of the home. Efficiency will become more important to you then getting an exact estimate of repairs. You will find that if miscalculating your repairs by a few thousand dollars screws up your whole deal, then your deal was too tight anyway.

YOU DON'T KNOW IF SOMETHING NEEDS TO BE REPAIRED

If you aren't sure about the condition of something in a house, assume the worst. Assume that it needs to be fixed. For example, if the utilities are off and you can't test a very old furnace, assume that it needs to be replaced. If you can't enter a home and it was built in the 1960's, assume that the bathroom needs to be updated. In other words, if you think that something needs to be replaced, assume that it does. Remember that your goal is not to get a precise estimate of the repair costs but rather to make an offer and see if the seller is motivated.

ACTUAL COSTS VS. EDUCATED GUESSTIMATES

Giving actual repair costs is not something that I can accomplish here in this course; however, I provide you with guidelines below that I use every time I make an offer. This is all that you need. If you don't feel comfortable making offers without knowing the exact repair costs, then you are not ready to move forward. I understand that this is difficult to accept, particularly when you are starting out and can't afford to make many mistakes, but I include a fudge factor in all of my estimates to cover any mistakes 1 might make. The bottom line is this. If the success or failure of your deal hinges upon the accuracy of your repair estimate, then your offer is too high and your deal is too tight. A few thousand dollars one way or the other shouldn't make much difference to you.

REPAIR GUIDELINES

Many of the following guidelines are printed in Chapter 10: Other Team Members under Contractors. However, they are included here again for your reference as they are relevant to the current topic as well.

HEATING, VENTILATING AND AIR CONDITIONING (HVAC)

Typically a HVAC company is going to charge anywhere from $35-70 per hour to come out and do repairs. If you ever need to have the unit for a heating system replaced, you can expect to spend approximately

$1200-$3200. At the lower end of the range, I have replaced gas forced hot air furnaces for as little as $1200 while new gas steam boilers have cost me as much as $3200.

HEATING, VENTILATING AND AIR CONDITIONING (HVAC)	
Repairs	$35-$70/hour
Forced air furnace (gas or oil)	$1,200-$1,800
Hot water boiler (gas or oil)	$1,800-$2,500
Steam boiler (gas or oil)	$2,500-$3,200
Oil tank removal	$500
General repairs	$300-$1,000
Central air repairs	$300-$1,000
Central air replacement	$1,000-$2,000
Central air duct work	$1,500-$5,000
PLUMBING	
Hourly	$35-70
Entire re-plumb of home	$1,500-$4,000
Replace sewer line	$1,500-$5,500
(Note: the deeper the line and the longer the run, the more this will cost)	
Sewer Line cleanout	$150-$250
Hot water heater	$350-$475
Hot water heater (do it yourself)	$250
Well Pumps	$350-$700
WINDOWS	
Replacement windows	$150-$300*

FLOORING

Carpeting isn't cheap, but you can get a wide range of pricing for the same product. Find out who works with investors in your town and determine if they have special pricing for investors. On average I can save about 25% over the lowest retail pricing in carpet stores by dealing with a company that specializes in corporate accounts.

Hardwood floors are beautiful and usually too costly to redo for low-end rehabs. On the other hand, in upper scale homes, hardwood floors add to the value of a home and therefore I will refinish hardwood floors, but only in my nicest homes.

I usually assume that I will be putting new vinyl flooring in my kitchens and baths. If the bathrooms have good ceramic tile on the floor, then I'll leave it alone. Otherwise, new vinyl goes down. Vinyl flooring is cheap and it adds tremendously to the appearance of the home.

FLOORING	
Carpet cleaning (minimum 5 rooms)	$30-$70 per room
Carpet installation	$9-$15 per sq. yd.
Refinish hardwood floors	$1.50-$2.50 per sq. ft.
Vinyl floor replacement	$2-$4 per sq. ft.

ELECTRICAL SYSTEM

Many older homes may need to have the electrical service updated. They may not have grounded outlets, and they may still have fuses instead of circuit breakers. Rehabbers will want to make sure all of the homes have updated electrical systems in order to pass inspections and meet the electrical needs of the new buyers.

ELECTRIC	
Upgrade service (breakers and amperage)	$800-$1,200
Rewire entire house	$2,700-$4,000

KITCHENS AND BATHS

These are probably the two most important areas when dealing with renovations. Most of the homes that I have purchased have had outdated kitchens and bathrooms. What many people perceive to be expensive fixes are really, relatively cheap. Money spent renovating kitchens and bathrooms is what gets a rehabber their best returns.

KITCHENS	
Cabinet replacements	$700-$2,500
Countertops and installation	$150-$700
New sink and fixtures	$200-$400
Total Kitchen Renovation	$1,500-$5,000

Note: While you can spend more than $5,000 on a kitchen, you can have a basic kitchen installed for between $1,500 and $2,000.

BATHROOMS	
New vanity, sink and cabinet	$200-$500
New tub enclosure	$200-$500
New tub and surround	$300-$1,000
New toilet	$200
Total Bath Renovation	$700-$3,000

Note: While you can spend as much as $3,000 on a bath, you can have a basic bathroom redone for between $1,000 and $1,500.

PAINTING	
Paint interior	$150-$250 per room
Paint exterior	$1,000-$5,000

Notes:

(1) I usually spend about $300-$500 on good quality paint and pay someone $300-500 to paint a home for me over the course of a day or two.

(2) The cost of exterior painting will vary with size of home and condition of existing surface. A good exterior paint job takes more time and is almost as costly as new vinyl siding. For these reasons, I prefer vinyl siding.

ROOF / GUTTERS

The amount that you will spend on a roof will depend upon the type of roof (flat rubber, pitched shingle, pitched slate, etc.), the size of the roof, and the extent of the repairs required. In my area, it costs about

$700 to lay a new flat roof on a small home and about $175-$200 per square (100SF) for a new layer of shingles on a larger home. If you have to tear off and replace the roof, these estimates go up a little bit.

Gutters can be expensive or inexpensive to replace, depending upon the type that you use. They can be bought in pieces and assembled, but unless this is done carefully and the seams caulked properly, the finished product has a good chance of leaking. When replacing gutters, I prefer to install the seamless variety, which run me about $3 per foot.

ESTIMATED REPAIR COSTS FOR SIDING

In my area, siding is an expensive proposition, particularly if there are no existing soffits. New siding can cost between $3,000 and $5,000 for a standard 1200SF home. Therefore, many rehabbers prefer to paint the exterior of the home rather than install vinyl siding unless they are in a neighborhood where most of the homes have siding already.

ESTIMATED REPAIR COSTS FOR SHEET ROCK

In my area, it costs about $25-$35 to install a 4' × 8' piece of sheet rock, depending on the amount you are having installed. Many times, gouges, holes and other marks on walls and ceilings can be repaired rather than replaced. Likewise, different textures can be sprayed onto ceilings and sometimes walls to cover imperfections. When estimating repairs, use your best judgment and when in doubt, assume replacement rather than repair.

USE A FUDGE FACTOR

Even after estimating repair costs on hundreds of homes, I still miss things that need to be fixed and as a result I underestimate my repair costs all the time. For this reason, I recommend adding at least 20% to your figure every time. If you don't spend the money that you budget on one renovation, you will spend it on another.

FIVE MINUTE "QUICKIE" ESTIMATE

In time you will be able to walk in a house, throughout the house, and out of the front door and have a realistic repair figure in your head before you get back to your car. My inspections go something like this:

- **Step 1 (Exterior)** - Check garage, size of lot, condition of roof and gutters, condition of windows (old or new, wood or replacement) and condition of exterior paint/siding as I walk up to the house and once around the outside with a quick check for cracks in the foundation and sags in the porches and roof lines. I also check the outside for a central air conditioning unit or a heat pump to determine the condition and age of the unit.
- **Step 2 (Interior - First Floor - House Locked)** - 1 look through the windows to determine the type of heating system. Vents indicate at least forced hot air and maybe central air conditioning. Radiators indicate some type of boiler, which adds about $1500-$2000 to my repair estimate since they are more expensive to replace than forced hot air units. I also try to check the condition of the kitchen. In my experience, if the kitchen has been maintained, then the rest of the house isn't so bad either.
- **Step 2 (Interior - First Floor - House Open I Key Available)** - I usually head straight for the kitchen. In my opinion this one room tells more about the home then anything else, if the kitchen has been maintained, then the rest of the house isn't so bad either.
- **Step 3 (Interior - Second Floor I Remainder of First Floor)** - Check condition and layout of bathrooms (need to

clean and update or totally gut) and floor plan of the house. Note paint and carpet, but these almost always need to be redone.

- **Step 4 (Basement)** - Head to the basement. Check to see if it's finished or not. Look at the type and condition of the heating unit (oil or gas and, if it's a boiler, steam or hot water) and hot water heater. Check the electric panel (if updated or not), plumbing (galvanized or copper), and type and condition of heating system.

This seems like a lot, but once you've done it a few times, it becomes second nature. Basically you are looking for are the big things, the stuff that jumps right out at you. On the exterior, you're looking at the roof, windows, paint/siding and foundation. On the interior you need to see your major systems (heating, plumbing and electric), and your kitchen and baths. It is pretty much a given that you are going to repaint and put new carpeting in every home, but you don't need to know the exact square footage of each home to come up with a ballpark figure.

It really isn't hard to estimate repairs as soon as you have done a few. Before long you will be comparing homes that you are inspecting to homes that you bought in the past and you will know exactly what needs to be done. When I wholesale a home, I usually ask my buyer what they think it will cost them to repair it. I like getting different perspectives from others and it gives me an idea of the buyer's preferences. You will learn what a wide range "repaired" means. To some people it is very little, to others everything has to be redone. For this reason, I tend not to estimate repairs for others or put a dollar figure on the cost of repairing a home. I let my buyers determine that for themselves.

PROPERTY INSPECTION REPORT

On the following page is a copy of a property inspection report. It covers all of the physical aspects of a property that I take into consideration when estimating repairs. You may find it useful when you perform your inspections.

PROPERTY INSPECTION REPORT

Property Address ____

Year Built ________

 # Bedrooms _____ **# Bathrooms** _____

Size of House ________ **Size of Lot** ________

1) **Grounds Condition** (include deck, driveway, landscaping, fence, etc.)? **Lots of trash to remove?**

____

2) **Exterior**

Does the foundation need repair?

____

Does the roof need to be replaced?

____

Exterior Type? _______ Repairs, painting, siding?

____

Type of parking, size and condition?

____

3) **Interior**

# of windows?________ Do they need replacing?

____

or rooms that need carpet? ______________________________

of rooms that need vinyl? _______________________________

Do hardwood floors need refinishing? ______________________

# of Bedrooms? ___________ # of Bathrooms _____________

Does the kitchen need replacing? ______ # of cabinets? ________

Do the bathrooms need cleaning, upgrade, or total remodel?

____

Is there a basement? _________ If so, is it finished? ____________

Is basement dry? ________ Does it have a sump pump? ________

Total # of rooms? ____________

What is required for painting?

____

4) **Systems**

What type of heat does the home have?
☐ Gas ☐ Oil ☐ Electric

☐ Radiator ☐ Forced Hot Air ☐ Baseboard ☐ Gravity

Condition of system?

____

Does the home have central air conditioning?

____

Does the home have circuit breakers or fuses?

____

Condition of plumbing?

____

What condition is the Hot water heater in?

____

5) **Appliances**

What usable appliances are included?

____

What do you estimate total repairs to be?
$________________________________

Could you enter the home? ________ Is it habitable? ________

What is the condition of the neighboring properties?

____

Comments:

____

____

What comp is most comparable?

____

CHAPTER 14

MAKING OFFERS

IMPORTANCE OF MAKING OFFERS

When I first started pursuing real estate, I must have looked at hundreds of homes and as a result, I didn't think that this business could work. Notice how I said "looked at." I wasn't making any offers. Needless to say, if you don't make an offer on a home, you aren't going to be able to buy it. You must make offers in order to buy.

RATIO OF OFFERS MADE TO OFFERS ACCEPTED

Once I started making offers and realized that this stuff really does work, I also realized the importance of making many offers to buy a few properties. When I first started, my ratio of offers made to offers accepted was about 30 to 1. This ratio improved greatly as I learned more about what I was doing. Today I'm able to buy about 1 out of every 7 homes on which I submit an offer.

Keep this in mind when you start to make offers. If your ratios are the same as mine when I first started investing, then assuming you're looking at 10 houses each week and only making 2 offers, it could be 15 weeks and 150 homes later before you get your first deal. That can be pretty discouraging, but if that is the pace at which you want to move, feel free to do so. If not, then you'll need to do one of two things — overcome your fear of making offers on properties with legitimate wholesale potential or do a better job of screening properties before you go visit them. You should be making offers on most of the properties that you visit, at least 8 out of 10 with the other 2 having a problem that can't be fixed (e.g., location, layout, etc.). The other thing you can do to accelerate your success is pick up the pace. If you want to do one deal per month, then you may have to make 30 offers per month. If you want to do one deal per week, then you may have to make 30 offers per week. Of course, most sellers are going to say "no," but you are only looking for the ones that say "yes". The bottom line is that the more offers you make, the more homes you will buy.

As time goes by, your ratios will improve as mine did. Your knowledge of local neighborhoods will increase along with your understanding of the sellers. For instance, now I know when an offer is more likely to be accepted than not due to the circumstances of the sale, and I have started pursuing the deals most likely to be accepted. The deals have several common characteristics, the first of which is that they are all VACANT. I used to make offers on homes that were still occupied, but not any more. Big waste of time. Second, usually they have been on the market for quite some time. Third, they may be brand new listings but listed really low. If they come out low enough, I will offer full price right away. Fourth, I target homes whose price has recently been reduced. And finally, in the neighborhoods that I like the most, I always pursue homes regardless of their listing price, offering what works for me. Some I get, some I don't.

DECIDING WHICH CONTRACT TO USE

Many new investors have difficulty finding a good contract to use when making offers. Some use this as an excuse for never getting started in real estate investing. They feel that they don't have the perfect purchase and sale agreement and therefore, they cannot make an offer. For all of those who are worried about the quality of your purchase contract, I'm telling you right now that the forms are not that big of a deal. If you really need some peace of mind, get a hold of a contract and have an attorney review it. Let your attorney know what your goals are and they will make sure that your contract will help you to accomplish your goals. However, keep in mind that though you want to have a legal and binding agreement, do not get hung up on having the perfect contract. A standard purchase agreement (an example of which is included in Appendix B: Forms) simply states the intent of the two parties involved and how they intend to ensure that their decisions are implemented properly. If one party intends to sell and the other party intends to buy, then the contract merely describes the manner in which this is to be done. When a contract can get someone into trouble is when the one party doesn't follow through on their end of the bargain. For example, if you sign a contract to buy a home and then back out, then the seller will revert back to the contract to find out their rights. Similarly, if the seller backs out of your deal, then you can revert back to the contract to examine your rights under the agreement. In other words, the only time that you ever have to worry about the language in a contract is when you don't do what you were supposed to do. If you sign a contract to buy, you should be prepared to buy, if you sign a contract to sell you should be prepared to sell.

Once again, I urge you not to sign contracts to purchase a property if you don't intend to settle on the deal if you can't flip the property. This is unethical, immoral and will come back to haunt you. If this is the only way that you can operate, I would suggest disclosing this to the seller and either signing a non-exclusive option to purchase the property which gives you the right to purchase the property but permits the seller to sell it to other people or, if you want to lock up the exclusive right to buy the property so you don't waste your time, signing a contract to purchase which includes a clause stating that you will not settle on the property if you cannot find a buyer.

One other thing to consider when talking about contracts is that even if the other party blatantly disregards their obligations under the agreement, it will be too costly for you to sue for damages unless those damages are significantly greater than the time and money you will invest in a court battle, particularly if you are dealing with a sophisticated buyer or seller. Also keep in mind that though you may win, you still need to collect the judgment. Of course, you can always sue for a huge amount and hope for a settlement, but why bother? Unless you've really lost out on a lot of money, say $100,000 or more, I would really think twice about pursuing anything in court. A more likely scenario is to try to reason with the other party and make an equitable arrangement acceptable to both parties. Otherwise, I would just let it go and start using my time to pursue other more profitable endeavors. In my view, time wasted in a dispute is time which could be used to do good deals or otherwise grow as an investor.

CONTRACTS AND LISTED PROPERTIES

Oftentimes, local custom will dictate the purchase contract that you use, particularly when you are making offers on properties listed through the MLS. Your local Board of Realtors probably has a form of purchase contract preferred by Realtors in your area which any Realtor will want you to use. You can obtain a copy by contacting any local real estate agent or the Board of Realtors themselves. In the event that you are diametrically opposed to using the local contract, you can cross out clauses and make changes to others, but realize that these changes may hurt the possibility of getting your offer accepted, particularly with bank-owned properties. Private sellers who have enlisted the services of a Realtor may be more accepting of your changes.

Personally, I have never found it necessary to change the standard contract for my state (Maryland). As I said before, as long as you intend to keep your word, the form of your contract is not really important and by changing the contract which most banks are accustomed to receiving as sellers of foreclosure properties, you risk your offer being set aside for other, more "normal" offers or perhaps not even entertained at all. As aforesaid, private sellers may not mind your changes, but even so, I've never felt a need to make changes to the standard Maryland contract.

LETTERS OF INTENT

Another, much shorter, form of an offer is a one-page letter of intent similar to the one found in Appendix B: Forms. Some Realtors prefer to use letters of intent rather than full-blown contracts when receiving offers from potential buyers because it dramatically cuts down on the paperwork in their office. Other Realtors will mandate that you use a full-blown contract and won't accept letters of .intent. Whether or not you try to use these is up to you. I normally submit offers on the standard Realtor contract for my area unless I know that a Realtor will accept a letter of intent.

CONTRACTS AND FSBO'S

In terms of including your own clauses and using your own preferred form of contract, you have much more leeway when dealing with FSBO's. You will be able to include clauses which you will not be able to insert if you are dealing with banks through Realtors, such as one that says your offer is subject to inspection of the property by your partner. However, let me reemphasize that your intent should still be to settle on the property. You should have a real-life partner and you should be prepared to settle on the home if they agree with you. You should also be considerate in having your partner look at the property as soon as possible. Most contracts give 10 days for an inspection contingency. Remember, the seller is counting on you to perform, and as an ethical professional, you should either produce or exercise your contingency clause as soon as possible if you cannot. If you feel uncomfortable putting this type of pressure on yourself to keep your word, then I suggest that you continue as a Bird Dog until you have more experience under your belt or more money in your bank account or both.

CONTINGENCIES AND TERMS OF YOUR OFFER

When attempting to wholesale properties, make one offer and only one offer. In addition, this offer should be all cash and totally clean or, if you don't have the cash yourself, contain only one contingency — a financing contingency (notice that you don't need to have the cash yourself in order to make an all cash offer). Forget about making multiple offers and forget about asking the seller to carry financing. This may work with FSBO's, but the vast majority of sellers that you will encounter will be through Realtors and they will only be asking themselves one question, "Is it enough?"

PREQUALIFICATION LETTER / PROOF OF FUNDS

A Realtor will usually recommend to a seller who lists a property with them that the seller make sure any prospective buyers are qualified to buy their property. This prevents the seller and the Realtor from wasting time with buyers who either aren't serious about making a purchase or don't have any way to obtain the money required to buy the property. As a result, most offers that you make through a Realtor, particularly those involving bank-owned properties, will require some form of evidence that you will be able to perform. In fact, just about every bank that I deal with these days requires this type of proof. Without it, my offers won't even be entertained. This proof can be shown in two ways — a prequalification letter or a statement showing "proof of funds."

PREQUALIFICATION LETTER

A prequalification letter from a lender (private or institutional) states that you are prequalified for financing which will allow you to buy a property. In addition to using these letters when submitting offers on listed properties, they might also prove handy in the event a FSBO ever asks if you are qualified to purchase their home (this has never happened to me, but I can imagine it happening sometime). Whether the property is listed or FSBO, however, your offer is definitely stronger with a prequalification letter than without one.

PROOF OF FUNDS

If you have the cash to buy a property, then you can produce some sort of documentation-such as a bank statement, credit card statement with a cash advance limit, or line of credit agreement-proving that you have the cash available for settlement, or at least unqualified access to it. This is called "proof of funds" and most real estate agents will require it in conjunction with all cash offers which don't include any financing contingencies. For example, if you submit a $50,000 cash offer for a home without a financing contingency, then the listing agent will want to see that you have direct access to $50,000 in cash. Bank statements or some other type of proof will need to be sent with your offer. If you can't provide proof of funds, your offer won't even be entertained.

Personally, I never make all cash offers. All of my offers have a financing contingency and I attach a pre-qualification letter from one of my lenders.

EARNEST MONEY OR "GOOD FAITH" DEPOSITS

When you sign a contract to purchase a property, it is common for the buyer to give the seller a deposit which shows the buyer's intent to act in good faith in completing the purchase of the property. This consideration helps to secure the contract and is usually provided in the form of a cash or check. It is not necessarily required by FSBO's, but will most likely be required when you buy a property through a Realtor.

As a wholesaler, you will be making many offers and may need to make multiple deposits. However, you want to conserve your working capital, so here is what you should do. Insert a clause in your contract which states that you will place the earnest money deposit in escrow with your attorney once the offer is accepted. When an offer is accepted, you will advertise the property for sale and collect the same amount of earnest money deposit from your buyer that you are required to place in escrow with your attorney. Then simply deposit your buyer's earnest money in your account and write a check to your attorney. This way, you never have to come out of pocket with your own funds.

Sometimes, the Realtor listing the property which you are buying will want you to give them the earnest money deposit. I hesitate to do this unless it's a really great deal for a couple of reasons. One, I lose control over my money. Two, I know I can trust my attorney, but I don't know if I can trust the listing Realtor. One investor friend of mine placed deposits for two properties with another Realtor. When she found out that he was trying to wholesale the properties, she relisted them! Turned out to be a big mess.

Anyway, my point is that unless it's a fantastic deal, I would really think twice about giving a deposit to someone other than my attorney.

MAKE LOTS OF OFFERS / KEEP THE FUNNEL FULL

What you do today pays off 4 weeks to 6 months from now. If you make no offers for the next 4 weeks, then you will experience a drought in the future. I have made offers on properties and never heard back from the sellers. Then 3 or 4 months down the road they'll call and ask if I'm still interested in their property. Of course, I might be, but maybe not at the same price, particularly if I've got a lot on my plate. These callbacks happen more often then you might think, so just because you don't get an offer accepted this week, it doesn't mean that you won't have it accepted later.

OFFER WORKSHEET

The Offer Worksheet is a basic and useful tool to help investors determine the amount to offer on a home. It provides two simple formulas to use when calculating offers, each requiring one or more of the following three figures:

1. After Repaired Value of the Property
2. Margin for Rehabber's Profit, Holding Costs and Closing Costs
3. Repair Estimate
4. Wholesale Profit

AFTER REPAIRED VALUE

You can determine this figure by taking 5 comps, getting rid of the high sale and low sale, and averaging the other three. I suggest this for beginners to make sure that their comps are conservative and not based off of bad information. Though many investors will tell you to always work with the high comps (as I do now), I suggest that you wait until you become very knowledgeable about the values of homes in a neighborhood before assuming that you can get as much as the highest sale. I also suggest that the five comps that you use be retail sales, not distress sales. If you use distress sales as your comps you can come up with offers so low that you will never have one accepted. Make sure the comps that you are using are realistic. When selling homes it is prudent to work with high comps. When you're making offers, protect yourself and work with an average but realistic comp.

MARGIN FOR REHABBER'S PROFIT, HOLDING COSTS AND CLOSING COSTS

This number can be modified to conform to the costs in your area. In the state of Maryland, we have some of the highest — if not the highest-closing costs in the country (2.5% transfer tax). As a result, I figure a bigger margin into my deals to accommodate for the increased closing costs. For example, in Method One I use 65% of FMV instead of 70%, and in Method Two I subtract $25,000 instead of $20,000. It won't hurt you to be strict with your numbers, but being to loose with them could.

REPAIR ESTIMATE

You will calculate this figure following your inspection of the property. On occasion, I will make offers sight unseen and just assume that the property needs everything. However, I do not recommend that you do this until you have an excellent grasp of what it costs to repair different types of homes in your area.

WHOLESALE PROFIT

This figure equals how much you would like to make when you wholesale the property to another investor. Generally, I like to make this at least $5,000. If I am less familiar with the area or a little uncertain about the after repaired value, I might make it $7,000-8,000 or more. Just keep in mind that as you increase this number, your offer will become more conservative and as your offers become more conservative, they have a lesser chance of being accepted. This is OK, especially when you are first starting. Better to have an offer rejected than to pay too much for a property. But don't worry. As you get to know your market, your offers will become more precise and more will be accepted.

OFFER WORKSHEET

List Price ____________ **Listing Agent** ______________________

DOM ________

Fair Market Value Analysis (5 comps, take away highest and lowest, average the rest):

Address ____

Sale Price ____

____

____

FAIR MARKET VALUE AFTER REPAIRS (FMV)

____

<u>Method #1</u>

_________ × 70% = ________ - ________ - ________ = __________

FMV Repairs Wholesale Profit Offer

<u>Method #2</u>

________ - $ 20,000 = ________ - ________ - ________ = ________

FMV Repairs Wholesale Profit Offer

The lowest of the two offers is the one that should be submitted for offer.

Amount of offer _______________

Terms included with Offer ______________________________

Date of Offer _______________

Response to Offer _______________

Whether you've just started wholesaling or have been doing it for a while, sometimes you will be tempted to offer more for houses just so you can get something accepted. Resist this temptation with everything that you have! Otherwise, you will put a property under contract which you can't wholesale and you will be forced to settle on the property and rehab it yourself. Now, rehabbing isn't so bad. You will probably make money. However, if you don't have the financial resources to sustain your business through a rehab project, I recommend that you do everything that you can to wholesale the property, even if it means little or no profit. You will be much better off.

MAKING OFFERS SIGHT UNSEEN

Several times throughout this course I mention that I occasionally make offers on properties without ever seeing them. I do not advise that you do this as a beginner, and in fact, many people would not advocate it for seasoned investors. In order to make offers sight unseen, you must know your neighborhoods and the repair costs in your area very well. The reason I can make offers without seeing a property is because I know the neighborhoods very well, and have already bought numerous homes in the same neighborhoods. Because of my experiences in the neighborhood I know what I can and can't pay for homes. Even so, you may be asking yourself why do I look at some homes but not at others. It really is very simple.

If a home goes up for sale in a neighborhood where I am used to buying and therefore know very well, I will always make an offer on it. Whether or not I go look at the home before I make my offer is determined by the price that the seller wants for it.

Let's just say that I have paid $50,000 for homes in a particular neighborhood and did well with them. I may want to pick up another for about the same price, and would be comfortable offering $40,000 (not $50,000) sight unseen. If the asking price of the home is $80,000, rather than spending time to go out and see it, I would just check the seller's motivation by offering $40,000 and waiting for a counteroffer. If a counteroffer comes back in the $50,000 range, I will go out to further investigate the home. If the counteroffer comes back in the $70,000 range, I would just let the deal go.

If the asking price of the same home was originally in the $50,000 range, I would take the time to inspect it before I made an offer. I might be able to pay full price if the home is in good shape and wouldn't want to let it get away because I was making a lowball offer.

If the home came to me priced at $35,000,1 would offer full price sight unseen.

I frequently experience all of these scenarios. In many cases, my low offers are used just to fish out the most motivated sellers and find out who will come back with a counteroffer that I might be able to negotiate down to my preferred purchase price. If the counteroffer is somewhat reasonable, then I will spend more time on the home.

REAL LIFE EXPERIENCE

Making a lot of offers is something that really works. I have bought as many as 9 houses in one day. In fact I remember the first time very clearly. Over the course of a weekend I made about 40 offers on homes. Some were FSBO's, some HUD properties, some Bank properties, etc. On the following Monday, no less than 9 of my offers were accepted. Not a bad ratio. Sure, I had 31 people tell me, "No, we aren't going to accept your offer," but do you think I was upset about that?

You must grow a thick skin in this business, you are going to be told "no" more often then you hear "yes," so get used to it. Play the numbers game and make a ton of offers. It works!

CHAPTER 15

OFFER ACCEPTED, NOW WHAT?

BEGIN MARKETING

Now that you've had an offer accepted, it's time to crank up your marketing machine. Run an ad in the paper, call your buyers list, put out flyers, go to the investment club meeting, and call "I Buy Houses" ads. Unfortunately, when you buy a home, the whole world doesn't automatically know that you picked up a new deal for them. If you don't let everyone know what you have available, you won't be able to sell the home. Once you get a home under contract, it is your duty as a wholesaler to make everyone who could possibly be interested in your home aware that it is for sale.

ALWAYS BE PREPARED TO CLOSE A DEAL

You should always have blank contracts and assignment forms with you. In the event that you happen to come across a buyer, you don't want to lose a sale because you didn't have the paperwork to fill out at the time. If I found myself in a pinch, I for one would write the contract up on a napkin, take a deposit and follow it up with a contract. However, many buyers won't be willing to do this, so just be sure to carry blank contracts with you as I do and you won't need a napkin.

START TITLE WORK

The term "title work" refers to checking the title of the property to ensure that it is clear and marketable. Title companies can check the title themselves, but many hire abstract companies to do it for them. The "abstracter" performs two main services. One, they check the historical chain of ownership (or "chain of title") of the property to make sure that all of the prior transfers were performed legally and that the current owner does actually own the property. And two, they check to make sure that there are no outstanding liens on the property. Any liens that are found need to be satisfied before the property can be sold to the new buyer (unless, of course, the buyer agrees to take title subject to the existing liens). Several examples of liens are mortgages, mechanics liens (for work performed but not paid for), and tax liens (for unpaid taxes).

I begin title work on all of my homes as soon as possible. I do this for a couple of reasons. First, it takes a while to get lien sheets where I live and you cannot record a new deed without obtaining a lien sheet and showing that all prior liens on the home, if any, have been satisfied. Second, in the event that I find a buyer who claims to be ready to buy, I don't want them to be able to use having to get title work done as an excuse not to settle right away. Even if my buyer is a cash buyer who wants to use their own attorney, I tell them that the title work is already done and my attorney will sell it to theirs. I don't allow my buyers to come up with any excuses as to why they cannot settle on one of my homes.

REAL LIFE EXPERIENCE

In my experience, simply running an ad in the paper doesn't always work. It is a very effective means of marketing, but sometimes not the most effective. For example,

I buy homes all the time, but I rarely scan the classifieds looking for a great deal. On the other hand, if someone takes the time to call me, then I might be interested.

Right around the tenth home that I put under contract, I ran into a snag and couldn't get the home sold. I ran ads in the paper and waited, and waited, and waited, but no buyers were forthcoming. I printed up flyers for the monthly investment club meeting, but struck out again. At that point, I decided to get on the phone and call everyone that I knew who invested in properties. On my fifth phone call, I spoke to a guy who showed some interest in the home. He told me that he would go out to take a look at it and call me back.

Three days passed and he hadn't called, so I called him. He said that he hadn't had a chance to see the property yet. So I told him more about the home and talked him into meeting me out there. He met me at the home and was totally impressed. We signed the deal right then and there. With only four days remaining until my contract expired and I would have had to default or buy the home myself, my persistence paid off. The moral of the story is that someday you might need to go out and find a buyer as I did rather than waiting for one to find you.

CHAPTER 16

MARKETING

ADS

In addition to placing ads to buy homes, you will have to advertise the homes that you pick up for resale. I have run all kinds of ads, short ads, long ads, specific ads, generic ads, ads that made me seem desperate, and ads that made me seem totally unmotivated. After having spent thousands of dollars on advertising, sometimes in as little as a month, I have yet to pin down one failsafe ad that works all the time. What I have realized is that I need to change my ads every once in a while as they tend to become stale. Repetition is a good thing for most advertising, but to advertise the same home, or what appears to be the same home, over and over again draws less calls every week. When I run generic ads and run them continuously (once a week), that tends to do very well for me. Ultimately, only trial and error will determine what works best for you.

SAMPLE ADS

There is no magic ad that draws hundreds of calls. Below I share the ads that have been the most productive for me, and I hope they work as well for you.

If one of my ads is more successful then any others it is the following:

123 Main St * 3 BR, $80k area, only $45k! Financing Available (xxx) xxx-xxxx

Another ad which I've used with success is:

Fixer Upper*123 Main St., $80k comps, only $40k (xxx)xxx-xxxx

Two ads that can help you to build your buyers list are:

Wholesale Properties, seeking serious cash investors! (xxx) xxx-xxxx

Or

Fixer Uppers*Cheap, All Areas*Financing Available, (xxx)xxx-xxxx

One other thing to note is that if I have a property for sale in a good area and I list the name of the area in my ad, then I usually get a lot of calls regardless of what else the ad says. These ads are very effective on internet classifieds. I recommend using as many free places as you can. There are programs that allow you to create full blown ads for your houses with multiple pictures and post to 100's of websites with one click. Short ads like the ones above generate a lot of interest, but oftentimes it will generate many questions. It is usually free to give a lot more information on internet sites and you should utilize them often.

HOW OFTEN YOU SHOULD RUN YOUR ADS

I only run my ads once a week. I don't believe in spending the money to advertise every single day. In many areas, that can be a very expensive proposition.

WHERE TO RUN YOUR ADS

The type of paper with which I've experienced the most success is my weekly shopper. Papers such as the "Thrifty Nickel," the "Pennysaver," etc. are papers that people tend to keep around longer. Though this may be contrary to what most other investors say, I can undoubtedly state that my best success came from the ads I've run in my local Pennysaver.

FLYERS

Occasionally, I will put flyers out at our local investment dub meeting. Each one lists a number of properties and offers very attractive terms. Every once in a while, I will sell a home as a result of distributing these flyers, but I wouldn't use them outside of my investment club. On the whole, I have found them to be ineffective.

SIGNS

Signs have been a very effective form of advertising for me. You can use cheap signs or you can spend the money to have them professionally done. I chose to have aluminum signs produced at a cost of $23 each. Whenever I put one of these signs in front of a completed rehab that I had for sale, my phone rang off the hook. I've never used roadside or "bandit" signs, but I imagine these would work as well.

PHONE AND FAX SYSTEM

If you intend to get heavily involved in real estate investing, it is important that you have one phone number dedicated to your business. This number should be equipped with a voicemail system and a professional greeting. When answering the phone personally, you should answer with a clear and confident greeting, mentioning your name and the name of your company.

In addition to your dedicated phone line, you should also have a dedicated fax line. This is a document sensitive business, so it is inevitable that you will need to use a fax machine frequently. If you do not have a fax machine readily available at all times, then you may lose a deal because of it.

This is not meant to say that you need a phone and fax from the start. For your first deal or two, you might be able to get away with using a cell phone and borrowing someone's fax machine. But after you've closed a deal, do yourself a favor. Have your phone lines installed and buy a phone and a fax machine.

TAKE CALLS PERSONALLY IF POSSIBLE

I'm not a big fan of allowing your voice mail system to catch all calls and then getting back to your prospects. By using an answering service, I was able to determine that 30% of all callers were hanging up when they got an answering machine or voicemail on the other end. That's 30 potential buyers out of 100 that you lose. Due to the volume of calls I receive, I have also experienced tremendous difficulty in getting back to everyone who has left messages for me in the past. It is not uncommon that I never get to speak with someone after they have called and left a message. At times, it seems almost impossible for me to get back in touch with some people when it is convenient for both of us.

For these reasons, I strongly believe in taking a call while the phone is ringing. You paid advertising dollars to get it ringing so you might as well make the best of the call while you have the chance. Pick up the phone every time that you are able. It just may be a buyer.

QUALIFYING POTENTIAL BUYERS

Once you have parties interested in your property, it is up to you to determine if each party is legitimate or if you can make them legitimate. The last thing you need is to have someone else who just ordered this course put your property under contract so that they can flip it to someone else. You must qualify your buyers! It is imperative that you know whether or not your buyers are capable of performing. If they cannot perform, you need to identify whether or not you can help them to be performers.

From my experience, most of the people who call on my ads are beginners who have never done a deal before. In many cases, they don't have the wherewithal to pull a deal off, and no matter how much help you give them, they aren't going to get it done. You can identify who is serious and who is not by asking a few questions, which I'll share with you in a moment. If you encounter a serious buyer who lacks some of the knowledge (e.g., he doesn't know where to get the purchase and rehab money), then you can put the deal together.

QUALIFYING PROCESS

The first question you should ask any investor is, "How do you intend to pay for the property?" This catches newbies off guard and they usually stumble. You need to be versed from this point forward. When they answer, you need to take control. If they answer by saying "cash," you need to respond by saying, "Where is the cash coming from? Are you borrowing the money or do you have cash of your own?" If they say that they have their own cash (bank accounts, mutual funds, 401 (k), etc.) or line of credit (home equity or other), you should make them provide you with proof of funds or a sizeable earnest money deposit or both. Assuming they want the house, neither of these should be a problem. If they say that they are borrowing the cash, proceed as follows.

Ask for the name of their lender. It should be a private lender (not a bank) whom you recognize as a proven source of funds. Call the lender to verify that they are willing to work with your prospective buyer and determine if they are going to lend money on the property and at what loan-to-value (LTV). Once you have assured yourself that your buyer will be able to obtain financing, get together to sign a contract and collect a deposit. Don't sign a contract until you are sure that your prospective buyer can get financing. You don't want to bind yourself to someone who can't perform. Furthermore, when you do collect a deposit, it should be large enough to reassure yourself that your buyer will show up at settlement. I collect enough to reimburse myself for my earnest money deposit and sometimes more, particularly if I've never dealt with the person before. After signing the contract and getting a deposit, start the appraisal process with the lender as soon as possible.

If you don't recognize the name of their private lender, then you can do one of two things. The first option is to satisfy yourself that their private lender will be able to perform by contacting them directly. Again, verify that they are willing to work with your prospective buyer and determine if they are going to lend money on the property and at what loan-to-value (LTV). Then sign a contract and collect a deposit.

Your second option is to line them up with one of your own hard money lenders. Once you have verified that your lender is willing to work with them, sign a contract and collect a deposit. At this point, depending upon the lender, you may also need to tell them that you will need a copy of their credit report and either pull it yourself or have them provide one to you. If you must pull it yourself, your buyer needs to fill out a credit application similar to the one in Appendix C. Then you can pull their credit, if you belong to a service that gives you the ability to do so (there are plenty of these on the Internet), or have someone that you know do it for you (e.g., a mortgage broker).

You should also get an idea of whether or not your buyer has any experience with rehabs. If not, you will need to hold their hand through the rehab process, making sure that they complete the rehab and pay off your lender. Otherwise, they may default on their loan and jeopardize your relationship with that lender.

PRIVATE VS. CONVENTIONAL LENDERS

If an investor is planning to get a rehab or construction loan from a bank, then beware. Due to the abusive and fraudulent practices of some investors, "title seasoning" has become an issue and most conventional lenders will not finance properties which are purchased and resold through assignments or simultaneous closings. Therefore, most banks are not a reliable source of funds.

Private lenders, on the other hand, understand the business and are more flexible than conventional lenders. Therefore, your buyers can borrow money from them without much of a problem. If you are not satisfied with a prospective buyer's source of funds, then you should take them to a private lender or not deal with them at all.

Personally, I will not wholesale properties to investors who want to get a bank loan. I flat out tell them that they're not buying my house, regardless of whether they are prequalified or not. Some people get mad when I say this, but I don't care. If they are prequalified or know the bank president, then they can use them to refinance or to finance their retail buyer. I've been burned by banks who have pulled out at the last minute, and I simply refuse to sell to investors who want to use them to get the money to buy my wholesale deals. I'd rather have an investor walk away mad now then be left holding the bag right before settlement.

STAY IN CONTROL

Basically, it is your job to qualify your buyer and make sure that your deals settle. In addition to staying on top of your deals after signing a contract with your buyer, you need to know exactly where the money to purchase your home is coming from and that this source is reliable. My preference is to take buyers who need financing to lenders I already know, since I feel more comfortable and it offers me more control. Whatever you decide to do, you need to stay in control and make sure that your deals make it through settlement.

TAKING BACK A SECOND MORTGAGE TO MAKE A DEAL WORK

There are times when the amount that a lender is willing to lend on a particular property isn't enough to cover the original purchase price + your profit + closing costs + rehab costs. Sometimes you will know this upfront. After speaking with your buyer's lender and determining the LTV percentage at which they are willing to finance the property, you can multiply this LTV percentage by a conservative after repaired value to get an idea of the anticipated loan amount. However, even after you make this calculation, sometimes a lender will come back with an appraisal which is lower than you expected it to be. In either case, your buyer will need to bring money to the table or you will need to take back part of your profit in the form of a "second mortgage." Just like the lender's first mortgage, your second mortgage is a note which is secured by the property. However, you stand behind the first mortgage holder with regard to payment. If the property is ever sold, the first mortgage holder gets all of their money before you collect anything owed to you. If the buyer stops making payments and the first mortgage holder forecloses, you will be wiped out along with any other subordinate liens.

Second mortgages aren't necessarily bad, but they are more risky. Given the risk of non-payment, I prefer my profits in the form of cash rather than a second mortgage. If I do take back a second mortgage, I name the terms and they typically mirror the terms of the private lender's first mortgage. Let's look at two examples.

EXAMPLE ONE: FULL CASH PROFIT

Say that you get a property under contract for $35k. The conservative after repaired value of the property is $100k, it needs $20k in repairs, closing costs when you sell will be $5k, and you would like to sell it for $45k. After talking to your buyer's private lender, you find out that he will lend 70% of the after repaired value including $50k for purchase and $20k for repairs. At closing, there will be $70k from the lender on the table, which is enough to cover everything-$20k for repairs, $5k for closing costs, $10k for your profit and $35k to the original seller. No one needs to bring or leave any money on the table.

EXAMPLE TWO: TAKING BACK A SECOND MORTGAGE FOR PART OF YOUR PROFIT

Say that you get the same property under contract for $35k, but in this case, the lender will only lend 65% of the after repaired value including $45k for purchase and $20k for repairs. At closing, there will be $65k from the lender on the table, but you will need $70k to cover everything. What to do? Well, you know that the original seller needs $35k, so that leaves $30k cash on the table. Now assume that $20k is placed into a repair escrow, which leaves $10k cash on the table. At this point, you are owed $1 Ok and closing costs of $5k must be paid. Ideally, your buyer will bring $5k cash to the table for the closing costs and you can walk away with the $10k cash that remains. However, every time that your buyer lays out cash, it makes them less able to buy another house from you. One of the reasons my buyers keep coming back to me is that I get them into my homes with as little cash out of their own pocket as possible. Therefore, in this case, I would take back as much as $5k of my profit as a second mortgage to conserve my buyer's cash. The other advantage is that the deal closes rather than falls apart as a result of a low appraisal or LTV.

MARKETING TO YOUR BUYERS LIST

As you begin to develop a large list of buyers, it will be very difficult to notify them all by telephone whenever you have a new property for sale. Therefore, I suggest that you get fax numbers and e-mail addresses from everyone. By doing so, you can send out information on a property whenever one becomes available or maybe keep in touch with a weekly list of properties, reaching dozens or even hundreds of people with very little effort on your part.

CHAPTER 17

BUYERS

DEVELOPING YOUR INVESTOR DATABASE is going to be one of the most important things that you do as a wholesaler. Your database of buyers will be the lifeblood of your entire business. Without a buyer you'll never complete a wholesale deal. Once you have a good database of buyers, you can really cut back on your advertising. You can notify everyone in your database about all of your new deals and delay advertising a property until everyone in your database has passed it up.

GROWING YOUR DATABASE

You need to grow your buyers list continuously. Someone may buy a number of properties from you today, but in time you may saturate even your regular buyers with all they can handle. At that point, you will need other buyers to fill the void left by the one who is saturated. Ultimately, your goal should be to develop a regular customer base. Personally, I have four regular, aggressive buyers who buy about 80% of the properties that I get. I either sell the other 20% to other investors or buy and renovate them myself.

DO ALL OF MY BUYERS NEED TO BE "ALL CASH" BUYERS?

Many people believe that all of your buyers need to be "all cash" buyers. I have not found this to be the case. If you have buyers who are creditworthy and possess enough income, then they don't need cash. You can provide financing for them by taking them to the hard money lenders who will fund your buyers.

Cash buyers are tough to find and very hard to pick up as loyal customers. Since they are in a position to do whatever they want whenever they want, they will buy their homes wherever they can get a deal and not just from you. Furthermore, they usually like to make the rules, so it is harder for you to control the entire transaction. In this respect, if a cash buyer wants to use their own title company, then I typically require a substantial earnest money deposit until they've proven themselves. All things considered, I do sell occasionally to cash buyers, but I don't have a single one as a regular customer.

INVESTORS WHO CAN AND INVESTORS WHO CAN'T

Investors that you come across will be from all different experience backgrounds. You will have investors who have rehabbed hundreds of homes calling you, to people who have never bought a home before. It is up to you to determine whether or not you will be able to do business with someone who calls you. The following three profiles of potential buyers are meant to guide you in this respect.

ALL CASH / EXPERIENCED INVESTORS

You can usually tell immediately when you are talking to an experienced investor. They know what they are talking about and get right to the point. They want to know the cash price of the home, the address, and how to gain access so that they can go out to see it. They may ask a few basic questions regarding number of bedrooms, style and construction (frame or brick) of the property to determine whether the home fits their profile and is therefore worth further investigation, but they won't waste time asking things like "How big are the rooms?" or "Is there a garage?" Furthermore, if they decide to purchase it, they will know where to get the cash if they don't have their own and they will not have a problem with giving you a deposit.

INTERMEDIATE INVESTORS

These are investors who possess some of the knowledge needed to put a deal together, but need help with the other pieces. They may need the name of a good contractor, or they may have good credit but don't know where to get the money.

You will need to evaluate each intermediate investor and their situation on a case by case basis, particularly if you are going to refer them to one of your hard money lenders. You will need to judge whether or not you think they can successfully complete a rehab project, even if they have good credit. Otherwise, they may screw up the project and default on their loan, damaging your credibility with that lender. If I don't think someone is ready to tackle a rehab project, then I'll tell them so. I'd rather be honest and tell them that I think they need to learn a little bit more before taking on a rehab than sell them a home and set them up for failure. If they are persistent and have their own cash, I may or may not sell the house to them. It's a judgment call, but if I did,

I would collect a substantial deposit ($3,000 to $5,000) upfront to ensure that they show up at settlement.

NOVICE INVESTORS

Newbies tend to have a script from a course that they got from an infomercial and will ask you questions starting out with, "May I please have your name?" Then they follow up asking dozens of insane questions about your home. I usually cut them off by the 3rd question and just let them know that my house needs work, I'm asking 50 cents on the dollar for it, and if they are interested and have cash, please feel free to call me back. I'm sure that I come across as unfriendly when I do this, but the bottom line is that people who buy wholesale properties don't need to know all of the details. Furthermore, I honestly can't answer most of the questions asked of me for the homes that I wholesale. I've never stepped foot in many of the homes and couldn't tell someone if there is a heating system in the house if my life depended on it, much less when it was last serviced. The homes are CHEAP, and that is what matters most to the wholesale buyer. They realize that the amount of your mortgage, the last time you had your furnace serviced, or the color of your carpeting are all irrelevant when you are buying a home at a deep discount. Therefore, as I said, unless the person asking all

the questions has a pile of cash and is willing to part with a substantial deposit, move on to your next prospect.

TYPES OF BUYERS IN YOUR DATABASE

REHABBERS (NON-CONTRACTORS)

Rehabbers tend to look for homes in better neighborhoods, and most prefer light cosmetic work. However, there are some rehabbers who like homes which are completely dilapidated because they prefer to just redo the entire home. Important details for rehabbers are usually the location of a home and the number of bedrooms. I've found that most rehabbers want at least 3 bedrooms. Though I have sold a number of 2 bedroom homes over the last couple of years, I have either rehabbed most of them myself and sold them to end users or wholesaled them "as-is" to landlords. Two bedroom homes are easy to rent where I live.

REHABBERS (CONTRACTORS)

Contractors are also a great source for buyers. They have the skills and the resources to fix the homes, but many do not have the money to buy them. If you have a home and can line them up with the money, then they very well might become a regular customer of yours.

LANDLORDS

Landlords tend to look for homes in the cheaper areas. This isn't always the case, but most of them want homes in cheap areas that need very little work which will provide them with a high positive cash flow in a short period of time. Landlords want to put a tenant in the home and start producing positive cash flow as soon as possible, and therefore they tend to stay away from big rehabs which will cost them negative cash flow every month (mortgage payments, taxes, insurance, utilities, etc.) for an extended period of time before they are ready for occupancy.

At the time of the writing of this course, (February, 2001), rentals appear to be very much in demand throughout the country. With the strong economy over the last 5- 10 years, many people have bought homes. The better rental housing stock has been depleted as it was converted to owner-occupied properties. There is a serious shortage of "good" rental properties in Baltimore, MD, and from what I hear, this seems to be the trend throughout the country. Lately, I have many landlords buying from me, and they want as many homes as I can get them.

Occasionally, you will find a person looking for a home for themselves. I can recall four occasions where I have wholesaled homes to people who bought the home and fixed it up for themselves. Bear in mind, however, that in this lending environment, these people will need to bring their own cash to the table. They probably won't be able to get a loan to purchase your property from a conventional lender and you will not be able to take them to a private lender. While it is OK for your hard money lenders to provide commercial loans to investors, most of them will not be properly licensed to provide residential loans to owner occupants.

MY FAVORITE BUYER

My favorite type of buyer is the person who has reasonable credit and a good income. They can afford monthly mortgage payments, but they can't always come up with a lot of cash at one time. Many have jobs and therefore don't have the time to find homes or learn the ropes, two needs that I help to fulfill.

Since they have decent credit and a good income, these are exactly the type of people that my hard money lenders prefer. Likewise, these buyers like to use my private lenders since they want to purchase homes with no money down and preserve what cash they have. Therefore, I will usually build as many closing costs as possible into the deal for these buyers so they don't need to come to the settlement table with very much of their own cash. As a result of my helping them to purchase homes with little or none of their own money, these buyers like to deal with me and they are also able to buy more homes from me.

The majority of my wholesale profits come from dealing with these types of buyers. I help them find a property, get their purchase and rehab money, get the home refinanced, and get it sold. And, of course, I help them to buy another one from me.

FULL SERVICE WHOLESALER

As a wholesaler, your job is to sell houses. Many of your potential buyers will have little to no experience and will have yet to develop relationships with hard money lenders, attorneys, contractors, mortgage brokers, real estate agents, etc. Even those investors who have already renovated several properties or purchased several rentals will need help in one or more areas. If you can assist these prospective customers in overcoming their hurdles, you will dramatically increase your chances of selling houses to them now and in the future. Personally, 1 provide houses to other investors as well as a full scope of services. I line them up with the money to do the deals, put them in touch with a good settlement attorney, refer contractors to fix the property, refer real estate agents to sell their completed rehab, pass on the name of a good mortgage broker to get their buyers financed or themselves refinanced, and so on. In other words, I give my buyers every reason in the world to deal with me on current and future transactions. This strategy also helps me to ensure that my deals close successfully since I maintain control of the whole process. I know where the money is coming from, who is performing the settlement, etc. Even after the sale, I make sure that my investors are successful in completing their rehab and getting the home sold. I want them to buy another home from me, and the majority of all the investors that I deal with become regular customers because they are successful when dealing with me. We discussed real estate agents, private lenders, settlement attorneys and all of the other people that other investors might need in Chapters 7-10.

KEEP ABREAST OF YOUR BUYERS' NEEDS

Your buyers list will become one of your biggest assets. I do maintain a buyers list, even though I deal primarily with a handful of them. At this point, I know who is going to be interested in a home immediately after I buy it as well as what they will pay and whether or not they are in a buying mode. I stay in constant contact with my regular buyers. If they haven't called me in a while (some call me on a daily basis looking for homes if they are in a buying mode), then I will call them to see how they are doing and if I can help them with something. As a result, I always have a feel for what is going on with them and with the market at large. Nothing feels better than knowing when you buy a home that it is already sold and all that you have to do to complete the sale is make one phone call. I now have about 50% of the homes that I buy sold within minutes of getting them under contract. I know my buyers that well and so will you.

REAL LIFE EXPERIENCE

In the first 45 days of the year 2001, as I am writing this course, I bought 27 homes. By February 28th, I decided that I was going to rehab three of the homes for resale and keep one for my rental portfolio. The other 23 were already sold. I was able to buy 27 homes and sell 23 of them in two months because I have a good buyers list, selling all 23 homes to seven of my buyers.

Most of my buyers are not cash buyers. They buy from me because I find the homes they like, line up all the financing, get them their rehab money, line them up with contractors to do their rehabs (in some cases, not all), and advise them through the whole process. Some of my buyers have been investing longer than 1 have, but because I spend much of my time looking for better homes, better money, and better contractors, I can provide value to them.

My average profit on the 23 homes was just over $6,000 per property. Most of my buyers know exactly how much money I make off of them, but they don't care. The reason is that I always put them into profitable deals and help them get out of them ASAP so they can buy another home or two from me.

CHAPTER 18

CLOSING THE DEAL

ALWAYS GET A CONTRACT SIGNED AND COLLECT A DEPOSIT

Once you have a buyer who is interested in a property, it is time to get a contract between you and your buyer signed. You do not have a deal without a signed contract. Let me repeat that. YOU DO NOT HAVE A DEAL WITH OUT A SIGNED CONTRACT. You need to understand this. In the beginning, it was tough for me to ask my buyer to sign a contract and give me an earnest money deposit. Since I myself wanted to avoid putting any money up when I signed a contract, I didn't feel right asking for a deposit from my buyers. However, take it from me. You must do this to protect yourself.

When I first started wholesaling after I stopped bird dogging, getting contracts signed and collecting deposits scared the heck out of me. I was shaking like a leaf in the wind when getting the first few contracts signed, so much so that I only got one check out of my first three deals. With the First one, I was so nervous I forgot to ask. With the second, I was too scared to ask. With the third deal, though, I finally got a check. The results of these deals were as follows.

The first deal didn't go through, and I had to Find another buyer (I got a check that time). The second deal didn't go through, and I had to find another buyer (I got a check this time, too), The third deal went through without any problems. The moral of the story is that you should always collect a deposit check to protect yourself. Even if you trust the person, you will sleep much better at night knowing that they have something at stake. My success ratio to date without getting a check is 0%. My success ratio at getting a deal closed after getting an earnest money check is probably around 98%. So, let me say it again, GET A CHECK!

If your buyer gives you stories about why they can't give you a deposit or why they can only give you $10 or some other nominal amount, make it perfectly clear that your home is still for sale until you have a check from them in the amount of $1,000. Why $1,000? I usually make my buyers give me what I put down on the home. If I can do it, then the way I see it, so should they. Most people who can't come up with earnest money on a home will not be capable of completing their purchase, and you are much better off letting them get away now than finding out right before settlement that they aren't going to be able to buy the home.

ASSIGNMENT AGREEMENT - ALTERNATIVE TO A CONTRACT

Rather than signing a contract with your buyer, you might choose to execute an assignment agreement such as the one in Appendix B: Forms. This is a simple one- page form that conveys your interest in a contract to your assignee. The consideration for transferring this right is outlined within the agreement and is known as the assignment fee. This is an extremely simple process, basically accomplished with the phrase, "I, (insert your name) agree to assign my rights in this contract to (insert the name of your buyer) for the sum of $X,XXX)."

ASSIGNMENT OR SIMULTANEOUS CLOSING

Whether you choose to execute another contract of sale with your buyer or an assignment agreement is entirely up to you. If you execute a second contract of sale, then the title company will perform a simultaneous closing at settlement (see Chapter 19: Settlement Procedures for a description of a simultaneous closing). The downside of this is that there are two sets of closing costs. The upside is that your buyer won't know how much you are making on the deal.

If you choose instead to execute an assignment agreement with your buyer, assigning your rights in the contract to them, there will only be one closing (the purchase from the original seller) and one set of closing costs. The downside is that your profit will appear on the settlement sheet and thus be known to your buyer.

In my area, closing costs are very high (2.5% transfer tax alone), so I almost always do an assignment. Furthermore, the majority of my buyers don't care how much I make as long as it's a good deal for them. However, as I said, there is no golden rule. Use your best judgment in determining what works for you.

MAKING A NON-ASSIGNABLE CONTRACT ASSIGNABLE

While you will probably be able to include an assignability clause in a purchase contract that you sign with a private seller, in today's environment, most banks will not allow you to assign their contracts. This is a result of the fact that they've been burned by investors who don't settle on a contract if they can't wholesale the property. As a result, they won't accept offers which don't include a non-assignability clause. However, there is a way to make a non-assignable contract assignable. What you need to do is make the offer in the name of an entity such as an LLC, land trust or corporation whose membership interest, beneficial interest, or stock, respectively, can be assigned or sold. Once your offer is accepted, go down to your state department and form the entity whose name is on the purchase contract. Then you can assign or sell your interest in the new entity to your buyer. In essence, you aren't assigning the purchase contract, but you are assigning or selling the entity which owns the rights to the purchase contract. The same objective is achieved but in a slightly different way. In terms of obtaining the documents required to form and assign/sell an entity, you should consult with an attorney in your area to ensure that you are using the proper forms.

One more word of caution. When you form the new entity, be sure that the registered name of the new entity is exactly as it appears on the contract. Otherwise, it will not match the name of the entity as it appears on the new deed prepared by the closing agent. Of course, a new deed can be prepared, but this causes unnecessary delays and may raise questions from the seller, who must sign the deed. Just take a few minutes to double check and get it right the first time.

MAKING A NON-ASSIGNABLE CONTRACT ASSIGNABLE - MY METHOD

Here in Maryland, I have started making all of my offers in new entities. If I am making an offer on a property at 345 Main Street, the buyer on my contract will be 345 Main Street, LLC. When my offer is accepted I immediately set up my new LLC. The process of setting up your chosen entity (LLC, land trust, corporation, etc.) in your state is something that you should research prior to submitting your offers and have ready to go. For me to set up an LLC in Maryland, I simply fill in the blanks (dates, names, dollar amounts, etc.) on my boilerplate documents (my attorney drew up the first set) and fax the Articles of Organization to the State Department with my credit card number. Though it took me some time to figure out the whole process, it is now very easy and I can form an LLC in less then 5 minutes at a cost of $100.

After forming the LLC, I start marketing the property to other investors. Once I find a buyer, I will transfer my membership rights in the newly created LLC to them. This is done in lieu of assigning the contract with the bank. As far as the bank is concerned, their buyer is still the LLC, the same entity to which they originally agreed to sell the property.

In terms of transferring the membership interest, I have an Assignment of Membership Interest and Substitution of Member agreement that I use over and over. Everything is simplified because the LLC's that I create are single member LLC's (my corporation is the only member, although any person or entity can be a member) which do not require operating agreements. Among other things, operating agreements usually set up the rules by which the members of the LLC must abide, including the means for its liquidation or dissolution. As a single member of a Maryland LLC, I have no need for an operating agreement (I'm not sure if this is true in all 50 states). I answer to no one else and make all the rules. Therefore, I can sell my LLC whenever I want and however I want.

Among other things, my Assignment of Membership Interest and Substitution of Member agreement mentions the following: 1) name and address of the LLC, 2) my corporation as the existing member and assignor, 3) my buyer or his company as the assignee, 4) the assets that are owned by the LLC (i.e., a contract to purchase such and such property (e.g., 345 Main Street, Baltimore, MD 21202)), 5) the consideration which I am receiving in return for transferring my membership interest, and 6) the terms regarding how and when I am to be paid. With regard to this last item, my agreement states that I am to be paid upon settlement of the property that the LLC has a contract to purchase. Once signing the agreement with my buyer, I give a copy to my attorney and collect a check at settlement, which is performed by my attorney in his office.

Creating and assigning the membership interest of an LLC is really very easy and once you've done it, you will be amazed at how easy it is. It works well for me because the cost of setting up an LLC in Maryland is very reasonable and much less expensive than doing a simultaneous close. In other states where the cost of setting up an LLC may not be so reasonable, I would recommend using the same technique but with a land trust or a corporation.

Whatever you decide to do, I seriously urge you to check with your attorney to make sure it is legal and easy to do in your state. I purposely have not gone into every detail with my method because I'm not an attorney and I'm not familiar with the rules regarding LLC's on a state by state basis. Therefore, I must reiterate that although I have told you what I do, I very strongly recommend that whatever entity you decide to use to make your contracts assignable (LLC, land trust, corporation, etc.), you should talk with your attorney and enlist their help in setting up boilerplate documents for creating and assigning the entity in your state.

Finally, keep in mind that this method of buying property is not for everyone and certainly not something that you should push on people. Always try to make it work but retreat to the simultaneous close if you stand to lose a deal. I never use this method if selling to homeowners, and I rarely use it for a first deal with a new investor. It is much easier to transfer an LLC to someone with whom you have already developed a relationship and maintains a level of trust in you as a result of previous deals that you have done.

ASSIGNMENT FEE - PAID NOW OR LATER?

When I first started assigning contracts, I was told to collect my assignment fee up front. However, in the course of wholesaling over 100 homes in the past two years, I have never received my assignment fee before the home settled. None of the sophisticated investors I have met would consider paying an assignment fee without knowing that they were going to get clear title to the property, and the only way that they can know this for certain is to be at the settlement table ready to walk away with the deed. As a result, every single assignment fee that I have ever made, whether it is paid in all cash or cash and a second mortgage, has been collected at the settlement table.

SECOND MORTGAGES

On occasion, I will take back part of my fee as a second mortgage. There are two reasons for this. One, it allows me to control the deal and make sure that it proceeds to settlement regardless of a low appraisal from a lender. Two, it allows me to help my buyers conserve their cash, which breeds loyalty among my buyers since I put them into my homes with little or no money down.

In conserving my buyers' cash, I try to stay within reason, structuring deals so that I can pull some of my profits out in cash as well. Remember you are trying to create win-win situations, which means that you should win as well as your buyer and that it's OK for you to do so.

CHAPTER 19

SETTLEMENT PROCEDURES

THE HUD-1, ALSO KNOWN as the "settlement sheet" or "closing statement," is a breakdown of all the costs related to a real estate transaction. It is important that you learn how to read one of these because they are prepared by humans, and humans make mistakes. For instance, you may have negotiated for a seller to pay some closing costs, say $500, but the person preparing the HUD-1 doesn't reflect this on the HUD-1. If you don't catch their error before the transaction is complete, you will end up paying this $500 yourself. Moral of the story — always check a settlement sheet before closing. Check the math and check it to make sure it reflects your agreement with the seller. Otherwise, you may find yourself paying extra costs and/or losing money which you would have otherwise made.

SAMPLE HUD-1

Included on the following two pages is an example of a HUD-1 or settlement sheet from an assignment which I completed. I purchased the property for $41,000 and assigned my contract for $4,000. My buyer borrowed $60,000 from a private lender of which $41,000 went to the original seller, $11,500 went for repairs, $4,000 went to me for my profit, and the remainder ($3,500) went for closing costs. My buyer only had to bring $430.35 to the settlement table. Immediately following the HUD-1 is a line item description of everything on the sheet.

OMB Approval No. 2502-0265

A. Settlement Statement (HUD-1)

B. Type of Loan

1. ☐ FHA 2. ☐ RHS 3. ☐ Conv. Unins. 4. ☐ VA 5. ☐ Conv. Ins.	6. File Number:	7. Loan Number:	8. Mortgage Insurance Case Number:

C. Note: This form is furnished to give you a statement of actual settlement costs. Amounts paid to and by the settlement agent are shown. Items marked "(p.o.c.)" were paid outside the closing; they are shown here for informational purposes and are not included in the totals.

D. Name & Address of Borrower:	E. Name & Address of Seller:	F. Name & Address of Lender:
G. Property Location:	H. Settlement Agent:	I. Settlement Date:
	Place of Settlement:	

J. Summary of Borrower's Transaction		K. Summary of Seller's Transaction	
100. Gross Amount Due from Borrower		**400. Gross Amount Due to Seller**	
101. Contract sales price		401. Contract sales price	
102. Personal property		402. Personal property	
103. Settlement charges to borrower (line 1400)		403.	
104.		404.	
105.		405.	
Adjustment for items paid by seller in advance		**Adjustment for items paid by seller in advance**	
106. City/town taxes to		406. City/town taxes to	
107. County taxes to		407. County taxes to	
108. Assessments to		408. Assessments to	
109.		409.	
110.		410.	
111.		411.	
112.		412.	
120. Gross Amount Due from Borrower		**420. Gross Amount Due to Seller**	
200. Amount Paid by or in Behalf of Borrower		**500. Reductions In Amount Due to seller**	
201. Deposit or earnest money		501. Excess deposit (see instructions)	
202. Principal amount of new loan(s)		502. Settlement charges to seller (line 1400)	
203. Existing loan(s) taken subject to		503. Existing loan(s) taken subject to	
204.		504. Payoff of first mortgage loan	
205.		505. Payoff of second mortgage loan	
206.		506.	
207.		507.	
208.		508.	
209.		509.	
Adjustments for items unpaid by seller		**Adjustments for items unpaid by seller**	
210. City/town taxes to		510. City/town taxes to	
211. County taxes to		511. County taxes to	
212. Assessments to		512. Assessments to	
213.		513.	
214.		514.	
215.		515.	
216.		516.	
217.		517.	
218.		518.	
219.		519.	
220. Total Paid by/for Borrower		**520. Total Reduction Amount Due Seller**	
300. Cash at Settlement from/to Borrower		**600. Cash at Settlement to/from Seller**	
301. Gross amount due from borrower (line 120)		601. Gross amount due to seller (line 420)	
302. Less amounts paid by/for borrower (line 220)	( )	602. Less reductions in amounts due seller (line 520)	( )
303. Cash ☐ **From** ☐ **To Borrower**		**603. Cash** ☐ **To** ☐ **From Seller**	

The Public Reporting Burden for this collection of information is estimated at 35 minutes per response for collecting, reviewing, and reporting the data. This agency may not collect this information, and you are not required to complete this form, unless it displays a currently valid OMB control number. No confidentiality is assured; this disclosure is mandatory. This is designed to provide the parties to a RESPA covered transaction with information during the settlement process.

Previous edition are obsolete Page 1 of 3 HUD-1

L. Settlement Charges			
700. Total Real Estate Broker Fees		Paid From Borrower's Funds at Settlement	Paid From Seller's Funds at Settlement
Division of commission (line 700) as follows :			
701. $ to			
702. $ to			
703. Commission paid at settlement			
704.			
800. Items Payable in Connection with Loan			
801. Our origination charge $	(from GFE #1)		
802. Your credit or charge (points) for the specific interest rate chosen $	(from GFE #2)		
803. Your adjusted origination charges	(from GFE #A)		
804. Appraisal fee to	(from GFE #3)		
805. Credit report to	(from GFE #3)		
806. Tax service to	(from GFE #3)		
807. Flood certification to	(from GFE #3)		
808.			
809.			
810.			
811.			
900. Items Required by Lender to be Paid in Advance			
901. Daily interest charges from to @ $ /day	(from GFE #10)		
902. Mortgage insurance premium for months to	(from GFE #3)		
903. Homeowner's insurance for years to	(from GFE #11)		
904.			
1000. Reserves Deposited with Lender			
1001. Initial deposit for your escrow account	(from GFE #9)		
1002. Homeowner's insurance months @ $ per month $			
1003. Mortgage insurance months @ $ per month $			
1004. Property Taxes months @ $ per month $			
1005. months @ $ per month $			
1006. months @ $ per month $			
1007. Aggregate Adjustment -$			
1100. Title Charges			
1101. Title services and lender's title insurance	(from GFE #4)		
1102. Settlement or closing fee $			
1103. Owner's title insurance	(from GFE #5)		
1104. Lender's title insurance $			
1105. Lender's title policy limit $			
1106. Owner's title policy limit $			
1107. Agent's portion of the total title insurance premium to $			
1108. Underwriter's portion of the total title insurance premium to $			
1109.			
1110.			
1111.			
1200. Government Recording and Transfer Charges			
1201. Government recording charges	(from GFE #7)		
1202. Deed $ Mortgage $ Release $			
1203. Transfer taxes	(from GFE #8)		
1204. City/County tax/stamps Deed $ Mortgage $			
1205. State tax/stamps Deed $ Mortgage $			
1206.			
1300. Additional Settlement Charges			
1301. Required services that you can shop for	(from GFE #6)		
1302. $			
1303. $			
1304.			
1305.			
1400. Total Settlement Charges (enter on lines 103, Section J and 502, Section K)			

Previous edition are obsolete Page 2 of 3 HUD-1

Comparison of Good Faith Estimate (GFE) and HUD-1 Charrges		Good Faith Estimate	HUD-1
Charges That Cannot Increase	**HUD-1 Line Number**		
Our origination charge	# 801		
Your credit or charge (points) for the specific interest rate chosen	# 802		
Your adjusted origination charges	# 803		
Transfer taxes	# 1203		

Charges That In Total Cannot Increase More Than 10%		Good Faith Estimate	HUD-1
Government recording charges	# 1201		
	#		
	#		
	#		
	#		
	#		
	#		
	#		
	Total		
	Increase between GFE and HUD-1 Charges	$ or	%

Charges That Can Change		Good Faith Estimate	HUD-1
Initial deposit for your escrow account	# 1001		
Daily interest charges $ /day	# 901		
Homeowner's insurance	# 903		
	#		
	#		
	#		

Loan Terms

Your initial loan amount is	$
Your loan term is	years
Your initial interest rate is	%
Your initial monthly amount owed for principal, interest, and any mortgage insurance is	$ includes ☐ Principal ☐ Interest ☐ Mortgage Insurance
Can your interest rate rise?	☐ No ☐ Yes, it can rise to a maximum of %. The first change will be on and can change again every after . Every change date, your interest rate can increase or decrease by %. Over the life of the loan, your interest rate is guaranteed to never be **lower** than % or **higher** than %.
Even if you make payments on time, can your loan balance rise?	☐ No ☐ Yes, it can rise to a maximum of $
Even if you make payments on time, can your monthly amount owed for principal, interest, and mortgage insurance rise?	☐ No ☐ Yes, the first increase can be on and the monthly amount owed can rise to $. The maximum it can ever rise to is $.
Does your loan have a prepayment penalty?	☐ No ☐ Yes, your maximum prepayment penalty is $
Does your loan have a balloon payment?	☐ No ☐ Yes, you have a balloon payment of $ due in years on .
Total monthly amount owed including escrow account payments	☐ You do not have a monthly escrow payment for items, such as property taxes and homeowner's insurance. You must pay these items directly yourself. ☐ You have an additional monthly escrow payment of $ that results in a total initial monthly amount owed of $. This includes principal, interest, any mortagage insurance and any items checked below: ☐ Property taxes ☐ Homeowner's insurance ☐ Flood insurance ☐ ☐ ☐

Note: If you have any questions about the Settlement Charges and Loan Terms listed on this form, please contact your lender.

Previous edition are obsolete Page 3 of 3 HUD-1

DESCRIPTION OF SAMPLE HUD-1

The first page of the HUD-1 is broken down into two sides, one for the buyer and one for the seller. Each side contains a summary of the participant's transaction. For the buyer, this includes the total amount they need (Section 100), the total amount which is paid on their behalf by a lender or some other party (Section 200) and the difference, which is what they will bring to the table or take from it (Section 300). For the seller, this summary includes what they are owed (Section 400), what must be paid from the sales proceeds (Section 500), and the net amount that they will receive (Section 600).

The second page of the HUD-1 details the settlement charges to the buyer and seller. Section 700 calculates the commissions due to the real estate brokers, if the property was listed. This section is blank on the sample because the sellers did not sell the property through a Realtor. Section 800 details the expenses relating to any new financing. Section 900 details any items required by the lender to be prepaid. Section 1000 lists reserves deposited with the lender for taxes and insurance. Section 1100 outlines charges for title work completed. Section 1200 details document recording fees and real estate transfer taxes due to the local and state government. Section 1300 lists any additional settlement charges. And finally, everything is totaled at the bottom (line 1400) and reflected on the first page of the HUD-1 on lines 103 and 502. Following is a line by line description of each charge for both pages of the settlement sheet:

FIRST PAGE OF SETTLEMENT SHEET

101 Price at which the property was purchased from the seller

103 Total settlement charges paid by buyer. From line 1400 (first column) of second page.

104 Assignment fee paid to me in cash at settlement by buyer.

107 Prepayment of property taxes by buyer from the settlement date to the end of the tax year.

109 Reimbursement from the buyer to the seller for their prepayment of the water bill.

120 Total amount due from buyer

202 Amount borrowed from the private lender by buyer to pay for the purchase, rehab and closing.

213 Contribution by seller for payment of water bill from September 14, 2000 up to October 30, 2000, the settlement date.

214 Contribution by seller to pay for ground rent from October 15, 2000 to settlement.

220 Total amount paid for buyer

303 Takes line 120 (total due from buyer) and subtracts line 220 (total paid on behalf of buyer. If this is a positive number, then the buyer must bring that amount to closing ($430.35 in this case). If this is a negative number, then the buyer will receive that amount at closing.

401 Purchase price due to seller

407 Reimbursement to seller for property taxes from October 30, 2000 through June 30, 2001, which they had prepaid.

409 Reimbursement to seller for water bill which they had prepaid.

420 Total amount due to seller

502 Seller's portion of the settlement costs. Taken from line 1400 (second column) on the second page.

504 Seller pays off the remaining balance of their first mortgage.

513 Seller pays the amount owed to the county for the property's water usage from September 14, 2000 to October 30, 2000, the settlement date.

514 Seller pays the amount owed to the holder of the ground rent from October 15, 2000 to October 30, 2000.

520 Total amount that seller must use from the proceeds of the sale to pay settlement costs, satisfy existing mortgages and pay other bills.

603 Takes line 420 (total due to seller) and subtracts line 520 (total due from seller). This usually results in a positive number and, therefore, cash to the seller.

SECOND PAGE OF SETTLEMENT SHEET

805 Fees charged by the private lender to inspect the property before he releases a draw from the repair escrow. In this case, there will be two draws.

808 Fee charged by the lender for him to wire the money to settlement.

809 Amount going into the escrow for repairs.

810 Financing fee charged by the lender. Can be percentage points of the loan amount or a flat fee.

1103 Charge for title company to examine the title work.

1104 Charge for title company to prepare the title insurance binder.

1105 Charge for title company to prepare all of the settlement documents (deed, loan documents, settlement sheet, etc.).

1107 Charge for title company to handle the settlement.

1108 Charge for title insurance.

1109 Breakdown of cost for lender's portion of title insurance.

1110 Breakdown of cost for owner's portion of title insurance.

1111 Charge for lien certificate, which shows any outstanding liens on the property that need to be cleared up before settlement.

1112 Charge for judgment reports, which shows any judgments attached to the property which must be cleared up before settlement.

1113 Courier charge and charge required to have someone record the documents in person.

1201 Fees charged by local government to make deed, mortgage and any releases a part of public record.

1202 City and county transfer tax (deed stamps)

1203 State transfer tax (deed stamps)

1204 State mortgage stamps.

1205 Recording charge for Assignment of Rents and Leases, a document which allow a private lender to collect rents for the property if the borrower stops making the mortgage payments.

1303 Payment of property taxes.

1304 Release fee to settlement attorney.

1305 Seller's payment of October 15th ground rent payment.

WHAT HAPPENS AT SETTLEMENT?

In the event of a cash deal, settlement is very easy. The seller signs a deed over to the buyer, the HUD-1 is signed by all parties, monies exchange hands and the transaction is complete. Takes about ten minutes or less if everyone is organized. If there a lender is involved, then the buyer has many more documents to sign. Once all of that is signed, then the lender or their attorney makes the funds available to complete the purchase of the property and the seller signs the deed over to the buyer. This takes a little longer than a cash deal since there are more documents for the buyer to sign, but not too much longer. Maybe an additional ten or fifteen minutes.

SIMULTANEOUS CLOSINGS

If you are involved in a simultaneous closing where you are buying a property and immediately reselling it, then the settlement process is just performed twice and there will be a HUD-1 for each settlement. The first time, you will act as the seller and the title attorney will collect funds from your buyer which are placed in escrow. The second time, you will act as the buyer and the title attorney will distribute funds from the escrow to the initial seller for the purchase price of the property. They will also cut you a check for your profit, which equals the balance of money in the escrow account.

If necessary, it is sometimes possible to complete the first settlement hours or perhaps even a day before the second settlement, placing monies and documents in escrow until the second settlement is complete. Though this is not common, it is possible if you have a title attorney willing to cooperate.

If you are doing an assignment, the closing agent should have your assignment fee recorded as a line item on the HUD-1. It may simply state "Assignment fee to Steve Cook - $5000". In this case, the closing agent would simply cut me a check for $5000 out of the proceeds of the sale.

If you are doing a simultaneous close, there will be two separate HUD-1 statements. The difference between what you collect as the Seller on the second statement (where you are selling the property) and what you pay out as the Buyer on the first statement (where you are buying the property) is what the closing agent will give you in the form of a check. Keep in mind that two settlements need to take place. The funds that are on the table from your second settlement where you act as the Seller will be used to satisfy your obligation on the first settlement as the Buyer. Whatever is left goes to you.

SETTLEMENTS ARE SIMPLE

All things considered, settlements/closings are really very simple procedures, especially when you are dealing with investors who are paying cash. Settlements get complicated when you have institutional lenders who require your buyer to sign about 100 documents. Even those settlements aren't really complicated, but rather just time consuming when compared with a settlement involving an investor paying cash for a home which usually takes 10 minutes or less.

REAL LIFE EXPERIENCE

A very large portion of my settlements have mistakes on the HUD-1. Sometimes the mistakes only amount to a few hundred dollars, but a few hundred dollars is a few hundred dollars. You wouldn't take that kind of cash out of your pocket and throw it onto the street now would you?

On occasion, the mistakes are in my favor, but I always have those corrected as well. I once had a deal that on the surface looked like it would have made me a little over $3000, but by the time I fixed the errors on the HUD-1, it only made me about $2100. One could say that I lost a little over $900, but making the corrections was the right thing to do. And besides, I would have had to give the money back anyway when the title company tried to balance their books and picked up the mistake. In addition, after bringing the mistakes to his attention, the attorney had much more respect for me. All told, it pays to make corrections in both directions, so you might as well do so.

CHAPTER 20

CONTROLLING THE PROCESS

USING WHAT YOU HAVE LEARNED

There is an awful lot of information in this course. It is almost impossible to use it all immediately, but the important thing is that you do use it. You will learn much more by getting out into the real world and doing deals, and this course provides you with all the tools that you need to get started.

STAYING IN CONTROL OF THE WHOLE DEAL

The reason you need to know so much is that you always need to be on top of your deals. You should always know where your deals stand. If you just collect earnest money deposits from your buyers and walk away from the deal expecting everything to fall into place, then you will be surprised when you discover that not everyone follows through on their commitments. I'm telling you this because many of the investors that you encounter won't follow through if you don't hold their hands throughout the whole process. Therefore, it is important that you keep abreast of details such as where your buyer is obtaining their purchase financing, who is performing the settlement, when it is scheduled to close, the progress of the loan process, the progress of the title work, etc.

With the volume of deals that I do, it is extremely important for me to stay on top of everything. Without attention, my deals can spiral out of control in no time. However, even with my attention, I need assistance in ensuring that my deals go to closing successfully. This is where my team helps me to make it all happen.

If you have the right team in place — a group of people who do their jobs better then you can do them — then you simply become the coach. Your job is to manage every person in your team, making sure that they are all doing their part. Before long, everyone becomes familiar with you and your methods, and they fulfill their team duties extremely well, like a well-oiled machine. Consequently, your job as a coach becomes much easier as you do more deals with the same team. On the other hand, if you are constantly changing your team members, then you will always be training someone new and dealing with the bumps and bruises that result from having someone on your team who may make mistakes simply because they don't know how you like to do things. The bottom line is that you should put your team together, make offers, sell homes, and manage your team well. This is the key to being successful as a wholesaler.

ANATOMY OF A WHOLESALE FLIP

Finally, I wanted to include a list, a summary, of all of the basic steps in a wholesale transaction. Here it is:

Step 1) Make your offer.

Step 2) Offer is accepted. Sign contract to purchase property.

Step 3) Start title work.

Step 4) Begin marketing to find a buyer. Market property to your buyer's list and place an ad in the paper.

Step 5) Come to an agreement with a prospective buyer.

Step 6) Qualify the prospective buyer, making sure they have the cash or will be able to borrow the money from a private lender (preferably one whom you've used before) to purchase your property. Continue to market the property while qualifying your buyer.

Step 7) After verifying their source of funds, meet with your buyer, execute a sales contract or an assignment agreement with them, and collect a deposit. The sales contract serves as the receipt for their deposit. Either handwritten or include typewritten verbiage somewhere on your contract a statement such as the following, "Received $(insert dollar amount) as an earnest money deposit on (insert date)" and initial it once you receive their deposit. You might also include their check number or write "CASH" if they give you cash.

Step 8) Submit both items — the executed contract with the original seller and the executed sales contract/assignment agreement with your buyer — to your title attorney and schedule a settlement date.

Step 9) Go to settlement, pick up your check, and celebrate!

REAL LIFE EXPERIENCE

When I first started in the business, I believed everyone who signed a contract to buy a home from me. I believed everything they told me and took their word. Often, I got burned; however, it didn't take too many slaps in the face before I realized that I needed to take control of the entire process. At that point, I decided to control every deal by lining up contractors, lining up the lenders, starting the title work myself through my attorney, and mandating that my buyers use my attorney. Before taking control, I estimate that about 25% of my deals didn't settle with my first buyer. Since taking control, that percentage has been reduced to about 5% of my deals.

CHAPTER 21

A TALE OF TWO DEALS

IN THIS FINAL CHAPTER, I am going to attempt to give you a step by step account, every single detail, of two deals that I was working on at the same time. Here we go.

On September 19, 2000, I got a list of homes and decided to go out and take a look at them. There were about 20 homes on my list, but they were all over Baltimore so I decided to check out the ones in the area where I have the best luck. By the end of the day, I had looked at 8 homes and made offers on all of them. In addition to making offers on the homes I inspected, I also made offers on 4 other houses for a total of 12 offers. Yes, 4 of my offers were made sight unseen, but my offers were so low it could have been considered obscene. The twelve properties were a mix of HUD homes, bank-owned homes and one owned by a private party. In terms of estimating values, I knew the neighborhoods very well so I didn't need to check comps.

Two days later, two of my offers were accepted. I put the first home (Home #1) under contract for $55,000 and the second home (Home #2) under contract for $23,000.

Home #1 was a good home except that it needed a lot of work. I felt that the amount of repairs was in the neighborhood of $20,000 and I really wasn't in the mood for getting into such a large rehab at the time so I was hoping to wholesale the home. The neighborhood was desirable (#6 on the Neighborhood Scale) and I estimated the after repaired value to be about $105,000. The bank was asking $69,000 for the home, but they accepted my offer (made sight unseen) of $55,000. After having my offer accepted, I drove to the home to inspect the interior, putting a lockbox on it before I left so that my prospective buyers would be able to get into the property without me showing it to them (by the way, I get most of my lockboxes from the hardware section at

Lowe's. You might be able to find them at another home improvement or hardware store or by checking with your real estate agent to see where they buy them).

Home #2 was also purchased sight unseen. My purchase price was $23,000 and the seller (HUD) was asking $30,000. I knew the area (a 4 on the Neighborhood Scale) pretty well, having purchased two other homes nearby within the past year for $45,000 and $40,000 and knowing that a nice home in the area retailed for $85,000- $90,000. Consequently, I knew that I could wholesale this property really quick.

I called one of my buyers, an investor whom I felt was the most likely person to purchase this home, and told him to go out and take a look. I also told him that he could have the house for $35,000 (a great deal in this neighborhood) but that he had to move quickly if he wanted it.

Most of the bank owned properties and HUD homes have master keys. On occasion, a buyer will have a key to one of the homes I have purchased so I won't have to meet them there or put a lockbox on the home. Fortunately, my buyer for this house was able to gain access without my involvement.

I called the newspapers the same day that my offers were accepted to get ads in the paper. I particularly wanted to place an ad for Home #1 because I wanted to wholesale that one quickly and it needed more marketing than Home #2. The ad I ran in the paper was as follows:

Catonsville* 4 BR $100k+ area only $60k. Financing Available (410) xxx-xxxx

Later the same day I received a return call from my buyer whom I sent out to inspect Home #2. He had made a decision to purchase the home, so we agreed to meet the next day and that evening I prepared the paperwork.

The next day, my buyer and I signed the paperwork and I collected a deposit check from him in the amount of $500.00. Since I was bringing him to one of my hard money lenders, we also discussed the amount of work that he was going to do to the house in order that I might put together a financing request on his behalf.

Upon receiving the signed contract for Home #2, I took the contract to my title attorney's office (a.k.a., escrow company, title company, etc.) so that he could start the title work. I also dropped off a check (From my buyer) for the appraisal as well as the financing request for the hard money lender, who always uses this same attorney to prepare his loan documents. Now, I just have to wait for the process to play itself out, get settlement scheduled, and pick up my check.

Over the course of the weekend I got a number of calls on my ad for Home #1. I didn't keep an exact count — something I stopped doing a long time ago — but this particular area is very desirable so I know that I had quite a bit of calls, many, in fact, from people who weren't investors.

I gave many people the address to the home, but I wasn't getting any calls back. By the end of the week, I still had the home and I had to place another ad in the Sunday paper. Home #1 was beginning to worry me. I had my hands full with rehabs, and I really wasn't in the mood for taking on another. Perhaps, I thought, I had missed the mark on my rehab figure. I knew the numbers were tighter on this one than

I liked to see them. Nonetheless, I submitted another ad and waited for more calls.

The next weekend I received a number of calls again. One person was really interested and someone who looked at it the previous week also called back showing an interest. I worked diligently with each of these two people, trying to get one of them to bite. Because of the amount of work required, one of the parties was very skeptical while the other party didn't think it was so bad.

In addition to working with these two investors, I returned the calls of all my other prospects and found another really interested party. Since he was a new investor who had never done a deal before, I actually went out to meet him at the property. He told me that he and his father, who had the cash, wanted to do a rehab and that this was the area where they wanted to invest. His sister had just sold her home, which was 5 blocks away and very similar to the one I was offering, for $135,000. Therefore, he felt that he could get $130,000 or better for this home after it was repaired. I didn't think so and I told him just that, but he seemed confident in his estimate. Anyway, he and I met at the home on two occasions. He took his father out for a third time without me, and they decided soon thereafter that they wanted to buy the home. So we met and signed the contract, and I collected a $1000 deposit from him. Since I already had the title work in motion, I suggested that they use my attorney and they agreed.

Two weeks later this home settled and I walked away with a check for $3714 from the settlement table. When you add this to the $1000 earnest money deposit that I received and subtract the $500 that I put down when I bought the home, you arrive at a total of $4214 profit for this deal. Not a bad payday when you consider that I spent a total of approximately 10 hours on this one.

About a week after the settlement on Home #1, we received the numbers for Home #2 from my hard money lender. He was willing to lend my buyer $40k for purchase and $12k for rehab, so my buyer was able to give me my $35,000 and use the remaining $5,000 to cover his closing costs. The $12,000 for repairs would be put into escrow at settlement and released as the repairs were completed. Several days later, we settled and I walked away with a check for $12,000 ($35,000 sales price - $23,000 purchase price). This was a great payday since I had only invested a total of about 1.5 hours into this deal.

As you can see, both of these deals were different. One was much better than the other, but neither was bad. Sometimes you will have to work harder than others, but sometimes the deals are really easy like Home #2. Not all deals will be home runs, but every deal that makes you money is a good one. The more deals you do, the more home runs you will make. However, keep in mind that you shouldn't always swing for the fences. Go for as many hits as you can get, and the law of averages will produce home runs. If all you ever try to do is hit home runs, you will strike out more often than not.

One final note. My buyer for Home #1 renovated the entire home and did a beautiful job. He and his father had it sold within 5 months for $139,900. Personally, I was surprised that he got that much for it, but a few others in the area recently sold for about the same amount. He was happy, I was happy, the original seller was happy and his new buyers were happy. Everyone made out on the deal.

APPENDIX A

GLOSSARY

ACCEPTANCE - the act of accepting an offer which results in a binding contract. AGREEMENT OF SALE - a written agreement between a purchaser who agrees to buy, and a seller who agrees to sell a specific property.

APPRAISAL - a market value estimate of real property, through the comparison of actual sales of comparable properties.

APPRAISER - a person licensed or certified to determine the market value of property. ASSIGN - to transfer one's rights and obligations under a contract to another party. ASSIGNEE - the party to whom rights of a contract are assigned or transferred. ASSIGNOR - a party who assigns or transfers and agreement or contract to another. BINDER - see "EARNEST MONEY."

BREACH OF CONTRACT - non-performance, default, or violation by a party to a contract of any of its terms.

CLOSING - the finalizing of the purchase and sale of a property.

CLOSING COSTS - the expenses incurred by the buyer and seller of a real estate transaction.

CLOSING STATEMENT I HUD 1 I SETTLEMENT SHEET - a statement used to itemize all of the costs for the buyer and seller of a real estate transaction. COMPARABLES - recent sales of similar properties used to help determine the value of a particular property.

CONTINGENCY - a condition within a contract that must be met before the contract can become legally binding.

CONTINGENT - dependent upon the occurrence of a certain event.

CONTRACT - an agreement between two or more parties that becomes legally binding upon execution by the parties involved.

DEED - a legal document that conveys ownership of a property to another party.

DEED OF TRUST - a legal document that conveys title of a property to a neutral third party, usually for collateralization purposes.

EARNEST MONEY or "GOOD FAITH" DEPOSIT- consideration used to secure a contract, usually in the form of cash or check. Given by a buyer to a seller upon execution of a contract, this deposit shows the buyer's intent to act in good faith. ESCROW - consideration held by a third party (usually an attorney) until the conditions of an agreement are fulfilled.

ESCROW AGENT (CLOSING AGENT) - a third party used by a buyer and seller to facilitate a transaction. Usually an attorney or a title company.

FAIR MARKET VALUE - the value of a property determined by current market conditions.

FANNIE MAE - Federal National Mortgage Association (FNMA).

FHA- Federal Housing Administration.

FINDER'S FEE - the fee a person is paid for their services of arranging a real estate transaction between two parties. A finder's fee is normally paid for finding a property for someone to buy, or for finding a buyer for a particular party.

FORECLOSURE - the sale of a particular property to satisfy the debt of a defaulting debtor. The proceeds of the sale are used to satisfy the debt to the lender.

FRAUD - the act of cheating or deceiving another party to gain some dishonest advantage.

FSBO - For Sale By Owner

FREDDIE MAC - Federal Home Mortgage Loan Corporation (FHMLC).

GNMA - Government National Mortgage Association HUD - Department of Housing and Urban Development.

LINE OF CREDIT- a particular amount of money made available by a lender to a borrower. Lines of credit used to purchase real estate are usually secured by real property.

MARKET VALUE - the price that a buyer is willing to pay a seller for a property under normal market conditions.

MORTGAGE - a lien against a property given by the debtor to secure a debt to a lender. MORTGAGE BROKER - a person who gets paid to bring borrowers and lenders together.

MULTIPLE LISTING SERVICE (MLS) - the network of real estate listing used by real estate agents and brokers. Homes listed in the MLS are exposed to all agents and brokers who are members of the network. In addition to current listings, the MLS also contains information such as historical sales data of properties listed and sold. This data is useful in completing a comparable sales analysis that can be used to estimate the value of a subject property.

OPTION - an agreement that gives a party the right to purchase a particular property at a predetermined price within a specified period of time.

OPTION FEE - the payment paid by a party for the right to receive and Option. PROMISSORY NOTE - a written agreement executed by a payor as their promise to repay a loan.

PUBLIC RECORDS - courthouse records relating to real estate and other topics (e.g., corporations) which can be accessed by the general public.

REAL ESTATE - land and anything permanently attached to the land.

REAL ESTATE BROKER - an agent who receives a commission by bringing a buyer and a seller of real estate together.

REO - stands for Real Estate Owned. Term used to describe real estate held by banks or institutions.

RECORDING - the act of entering legal documents into public record for the purpose of notifying anyone who may be interested of the rights and claims of the parties within the recorded instruments.

TIME IS OF THE ESSENCE - a requirement of punctual performance stipulated in most contracts including those used in real estate transactions.

VA - Veterans Administration

APPENDIX B

FORMS

Forms can be downloaded from our website *www.FlippingHomes.com*

DISCLOSURE

The forms contained in this publication are intended for instructional purposes only. They are offered with the understanding that neither the publisher nor the author is engaged in rendering legal, tax or other professional services and that these forms should be reviewed by an attorney before being used by the reader. If legal, tax or other expert assistance is required, including but not limited to the review of these forms, the services of a competent professional should be sought (from a Declaration of Principles jointly adopted by a committee of the American Bar Association and a committee of the Publishers Association).

LETTER OF INTENT

This Letter of Intent specifies general terms under which the Buyer may have interest in purchasing the specified property from the Seller. Should the Seller find the proposed terms generally acceptable, the Buyer may then direct the Agent to prepare a formal Residential Contract of Sale for the consideration by the Seller. This Letter of Intent is not an offer to purchase or to sell, as such an offer shall be made only on a standard contract from which shall also include those provisions required by law.

- Property Address:
- Buyers Name:
- Purchase Price:
- Earnest Money: $
- Settlement Date:
- Financing Contingency:
- Additional Contingencies:
- Other Terms:
- This Letter of Intent expires 48 hours from the date of this letter.

Submitted for consideration this ______ day of _________, _________

_____________________ _____________________

Buyer Buyer

REAL ESTATE SALES CONTRACT

Seller, ____

agrees to sell to

Buyer, ____

the real property set forth below and all improvements thereon (Property), and Buyer agrees to purchase said Property from the Seller according to the terms and conditions in this contract.

LEGAL DESCRIPTION:

____

____

ALSO KNOWN AS THE FOLLOWING ADDRESS:

____

____

PURCHASE PRICE : ____

as follows:

(a) Initial Deposit $ ___________

(b) Sum due at closing (not including proration's) $ ___________

(c) Proceeds from a new note and mortgage to be given by Buyer or any lender other than the Seller (new loan) $ ___________

(d) Existing mortgage on the Property which shall remain on the Property $ ___________

(e) Balance due the Seller by promissory note from the Buyer as detailed in this contract (seller financing) $___________

(f) **TOTAL PURCHASE PRICE $** ___________

IT IS AGREED that the Property will be conveyed by a General Warranty Deed, with release of dower and homestead rights.

THE SELLER WILL PAY FOR: Revenue stamps (State, county and local); Title commitment in the amount of the purchase price from a title insurance company to be selected by Seller in the County of the Property location; Title abstract; Title opinion letter; Satisfaction of mortgage and recording fee.

THE BUYER WILL PAY FOR: Recording fees, prepaid insurance, prepaid taxes, prepaid interest, termite Inspection, appraisal fee, survey, fees associated with the procurement of financing, Property inspection, all other closing fees charged by the title company.

TITLE AND TITLE INSURANCE: Within 15 days from Effective Date, Seller shall, at Seller's expense, deliver to Buyer or Buyer's attorney, a title insurance commitment with fee owner's title policy premium to be paid by Seller at closing.

PRORATED ITEMS: All rents, water taxes or charges, taxes, assessments, monthly mortgage insurance premiums, fuel, prepaid service contracts and interest on existing mortgages shall be prorated as of the date of closing. If Buyer is to accept the Property subject to an existing mortgage requiring an escrow deposit for taxes, insurance and/or other items, all escrow payments required to be made up to the time of closing shall be made to the escrow holder at Seller's expense and said escrow balance shall be assigned to the Buyer, without compensation to the Seller, it being expressly understood that said escrow balance is included in the Total Purchase Price. All mortgage payments required of Seller to be made shall be current as of the time of closing. If the exact amount of real estate taxes cannot be ascertained at the time of closing, Seller agrees to prorate said taxes on the basis of the actual tax bill when issued.

THE DATE OF THIS CONTRACT ("Effective Date") shall be the date when the last one of Seller and Buyer has signed this offer.

EXAMINATION OF TITLE AND TIME OF CLOSING: If the title evidence and survey as specified above disclose that Seller is vested with fee simple title to the Property (subject only to the permitted exceptions set forth above acceptable to Buyer), and unless extended by other provisions of this Contract, this sale shall be closed on or before ________________ at the office of the attorney or other closing agent designated by Seller. If title evidence or survey reveal any defect or condition, which is not acceptable to Buyer, the Buyer shall, within 15 days notify the Seller of such title defects and Seller agrees to use reasonable efforts to remedy such defects and shall have 30 days to do so. Seller agrees to pay for and clear all delinquent taxes, liens and other encumbrances, unless the parties otherwise agree. Seller agrees to deliver good and insurable title to the property within 60 days of the effective date.

DEFAULT BY BUYER: If Buyer fails to perform the agreements of this contract, Seller may retain as liquidated damages and not as a penalty all of the initial deposit specified in paragraph 1 (a) above, it being agreed that this is Seller's exclusive remedy.

DEFAULT BY SELLER: If Seller fails to perform any of the agreements of this contract, all deposits made by Buyer shall be returned to Buyer on demand, plus reimbursement for any expenses incurred under paragraph (4).

ATTORNEY FEES AND COSTS: If any litigation is instituted with respect to enforcement of the terms of this contract, the prevailing party shall be entitled to recover all costs incurred, including, but not limited to reasonable attorney fees and court cost.

RISK OF LOSS OR DAMAGE: Risk of loss or damage to the Property by any cause is retained by the seller until closing.

CONDITION OF THE PROPERTY: Seller agrees to deliver the Property to Buyer in its present condition, ordinary wear and tear excepted, and further certifies and represents that Seller knows of no latent defect in the Property. All heating, cooling, plumbing, electrical, sanitary systems and appliances shall be in good working order at the time of closing. Seller represents and warrants that the personal property conveyed with the premises shall be the same property inspected by Buyer and that no substitutions will be made without the Buyer's written consent. Buyer may also inspect or cause to be inspected the foundation, roof, supports or structural members of all improvements located upon the Property. If any such system, appliance, roof, foundation or structural member shall be found defective, and the costs of such repairs shall exceed 10% of the total purchase price, Buyer may, at his option, elect to terminate this contract and receive the full refund of all deposits and other sums tendered hereunder. In addition, seller agrees to remove all debris from the Property by date of possession.

OCCUPANCY: Seller shall deliver possession to Buyer no later than the closing date unless otherwise stated herein. Seller represents that there are no persons occupying the Property except the following tenants of the Seller:

____

____

____

Seller agrees to deliver exclusive occupancy of the Property to Buyer at the time of closing unless otherwise specifically stated herein. Seller agrees to provide true and accurate copies of all written leases to Buyer within 5 days after the date of acceptance of this contract. Said leases are subject to Buyer's approval. Seller shall provide such letters notifying tenants to pay rent to the Buyer after closing as Buyer may reasonably request. Seller warrants that any rent rolls and other income and expense data provided to Buyer are complete and accurate, all of which must be acceptable to buyer.

[ ] MORTGAGE OR THIRD PARTY FINANCING: According to paragraph 1(d) of this contract, it is agreed that Buyer will require a new mortgage loan to finance this purchase. The application for this mortgage will be made with a lender acceptable to Buyer, and unless a mortgage loan acceptable to Buyer is approved without contingencies other than those specified in this contract within 10 (ten) days from the date of acceptance of this contract, Buyer shall have the right to terminate this contract and at that time all sums deposited by Buyer shall be returned to Buyer and Buyer shall return any surveys and copies of leases received from Seller. Seller acknowledges that there is a new institutional mortgage

being placed on the property and closing may be reasonably extended to accommodate the mortgage financing process.

[ ] SELLER FINANCING: According to paragraph 1(e) above, it is understood that the Buyer will execute and deliver at the closing a Promissory Note to Seller which shall provide for full or partial prepayment without penalty and shall bear interest at the rate of ____________ per annum beginning on ____________ in the amount of __________ per month such that the amount of such payments shall amortize the debt due in ___________ with all unpaid principal and interest due upon the last payment date, APPROXIMATELY ___________. The said Promissory Note shall be secured by a mortgage acceptable to Buyer and providing for the full and free right of the mortgagor to transfer the Property, in whole or in part, subject to the mortgage; and the right of first refusal to the mortgagor if the mortgagee shall at any time sell its interest at a discount; future advances at the option of the mortgagee

TERMITE INSPECTION: Buyer shall be furnished at Buyers expense, an inspection report showing all buildings on the Property to be free and clear from visible infestation and free from visible dry or wet rot damage by termites and other wood-destroying organisms. This inspection report is to be furnished by a licensed pest control firm. If a report shows such visible infestation or damage, Seller shall pay all costs of treatment of such infestation and all costs of repair of such damage. If the costs of treatment and repair shall exceed 3% of the total price, Seller may elect not to make such treatment and repairs and Buyer may elect to take the Property in its then condition or, at Buyer's option, to deduct the cost of repairs from the total purchase price and complete the transaction Buyer may terminate this contract and receive a full refund of all deposits made buyer hereunder.

ZONING: Unless the property is properly zoned for residential and there are no deed restrictions against such use at the time of closing, the Buyer shall have the right to terminate this contract and receive a full refund of all deposits made by Buyer hereunder.

LEGAL USE: Seller represents and warrants to Buyer that all improvements on said Property conforms to all building codes and restrictions that may be imposed by any governmental agency either national, state or local or from a Home Owners Association, Seller also warrants that there are no building code violations on the Property and that Seller has received no notice of any building code violations for the past ten years that have not been fully corrected.

PERSONAL PROPERTY INCLUDED IN THE PURCHASE PRICE: (Strike items not applicable): storm and screen doors and windows; awnings; outdoor television antenna; wall-to wall, hallway and stair carpeting; window shades and draperies and supporting fixtures; venetian blinds; window treatments; electric, plumbing and other fixtures as installed; water softener; attached shelving; hardware; trees and shrubs; refrigerator; stove; air conditioner; any existing ceiling fans, and such other items as is listed on a rider attached hereto or below, all of which personal property is unencumbered and owned by Seller.

THIS OFFER SHALL TERMINATE if not accepted

before ______ o'clock pm, _______________

R.E.S.P.A. COMPLIANCE: Seller agrees to make all disclosures and do all things necessary to comply with the provisions of the Real Estate Settlement Procedure Act of 1974 if it is applicable to this transaction.

ADDITIONAL TERMS AND CONDITIONS:

(a) Where the context requires, the terms Seller and Buyer shall include the masculine as well as the feminine and the singular as well as the plural.

(b) There are no agreements, promises, or understandings between the parties except as specifically set forth in this contract. No alterations or changes shall be made to this contract unless the same are in writing and signed or initialed by the parties hereto.

(c) The provisions of this contract shall survive the closing and shall not merge in any deed or conveyance herein.

(d) This agreement shall be construed under the laws of the State of ____________________

(e) A faxed copy of this signed agreement shall constitute a legally binding agreement.

(f) other

NOTICES: Any notices required to be given herein shall be sent to the parties listed below at their respective addresses either by personal delivery or by certified mail-return receipt requested. Such notice shall be effective upon delivery or mailing.

TYPEWRITTEN OR HANDWRITTEN PROVISIONS: Typewritten or handwritten provisions inserted herein or attached hereto as addenda shall control all printed provisions of contract in conflict therewith.

________________________________ date ____________

BUYER

________________________________ date ____________

BUYER

________________________________ date ____________

SELLER

________________________________ date ____________

SELLER

ASSIGNMENT OF CONTRACT

In consideration for the sum of ______________________________

______________________________ ($______________) and other good and valuable consideration, ______________________________,

Assignor, hereby assigns, transfers and sets over to

______________________________,

Assignee, all right, title and interest in and to the following described contract:

____

(Address)

dated ____________________.

The Assignor warrants and represents that said contract is in full force and effect and is fully assignable.

The Assignee hereby assumes and agrees to perform all obligations of the Assignor under the contract and guarantees to hold the Assignor harmless from any claim or demand made thereunder.

Signed under seal this ____ day of __________, ____.

____________________	____________________
Witness	Assignor
____________________	____________________
Witness	Assignee

APPENDIX C

CREDIT APPLICATION

CREDIT APPLICATION

Name: ____

Address: ____

____

____

Previous Address*: ____________________________________

____

____

Birthdate: ____

Social Security Number: _______________________________

Signature: ____________________________

\- Only necessary if they've been at their current address less than two years.

Made in the USA
Middletown, DE
08 May 2018